The
SEVEN

SECRETS

of

HIGHLY
EFFECTIVE
LEADERS

• • • • • • •

Robin Stuart-Kotze

Tellwell Talent
www.tellwell.ca

ISBN
978-1-77370-553-8 (Hardcover)
978-1-77370-552-1 (Paperback)
978-1-77370-554-5 (eBook)

To

George Campbell

Randy Findlay

Colin Patey

Three outstanding leaders with whom
I have had the immense pleasure of working,
from whom I've learned a lot,
and whose wisdom and friendship I cherish

TABLE OF CONTENTS

INTRODUCTION

The Harvard professor, Fritz Roethlisberger, used to tell his classes, "It ain't what you don't know that gets you into trouble, it's what you know that ain't so".

Everything in this book is established fact. It's taken from hard, documented research, and if you're interested, all the research is listed in the endnotes.

Stanford professor Jeffrey Pfeffer says that what people have been led to believe about leadership "is based more on hope than reality, on wishes rather than data, on beliefs instead of science".[1]

The information in this book is based on

- reality, not hope,
- research fact, not wishes,
- scientific proof, not beliefs.

Getting leadership right is important. Research shows that human capital – i.e. people – accounts for upwards of 80% of the market value of companies in the S&P 500.[2] Humans are immensely creative, and they have energy, thoughts and abilities which they can choose to use in various ways. But that choice depends on how they're led.

In 2014, SAP, in collaboration with the research firm Oxford Economics, conducted a global survey of 2700 executives about the skills that will be most needed in the workforce of the 21st century.[3] The top priorities are (1) ability to work creatively with others, (2) relationship building, and (3) cultural sensitivity and empathy - all things at the heart of effective leadership.

The outline of the book

The seven secrets of leadership are about:

- **Secret 1: Influence.** Leadership is not about position or authority, it's about Influencing the perceptions and actions of people. (Chapter 1)

- **Secret 2: Behaviour** (what you do). Behaviour drives performance. It's what you do that matters, not what you are or who you are. (Chapter 2)

- **Secret 3: The situation.** Every situation is different and requires different behaviour. You will be much more effective in your job if your behaviour is tailored to the specific needs of your job. (Chapter 4)

- **Secret 4: Motivation.** Unless people find their job, or at least some aspects of it, motivating, it's unlikely they will be successful at it. There is a set of powerful motivators that you can use both in terms of boosting yourself and others. *(Chapter 5)*

- **Secret 5: Culture and values.** Culture is "the way we do things around here". It's a set of largely unwritten rules of behaviour that define what gets rewarded, what gets punished, and what gets overlooked – i.e. what results in leadership or job failure. (Chapter 6)

- **Secret 6: Making teams productive.** A lot of work is done in teams and how you work in team settings is a key factor in leadership. (Chapter 7)

- **Secret 7: Handling pressure and stress.** In the fast-moving world of the 21st century very few jobs are free of pressure and stress and how you react to it can make the difference between leadership or failure. The negative effect of performance hindering behaviours is *five times greater* than the effect of positive actions.[4] People remember negative interactions with their boss more often, in more detail, and in more intensity, than they do positive ones.[5] *(Chapter 8)*

*You're wondering what happened to Chapter 3. It's a **non**-secret for highly effective leadership.*

- **Chapter 3** is about why highly effective leadership is **not** about personality. The reason it isn't about personality is because personality only predicts, at most, 15% of behaviour, and behaviour (how you act) determines your effectiveness.

- **Appendix:** The appendix addresses some of the most destructive myths about leadership. We've limited it to ten but no doubt you know lots more and we'd love to hear from you about what they are.

Your thoughts

In his excellent and important book, *Dialogue Gap*, Peter Nixon says" A leader's ability to dialogue effectively will help him or her handle complexity at the speed it arises, harness the creative ideas of (others), co-create with others, and remain dexterous to deal with change".[6] The world is changing at an increasingly rapid pace. As the Red Queen in Alice in Wonderland said, "it takes all the running you can do to keep in the same place. If you want to get somewhere else, you must run at least twice as fast". There is a clear need for dialogue and I would like to know what you think about the changing needs of effective leadership. What are the issues on which we should focus and which we should be addressing? If you'd like to enter a dialogue, my email address for this is kotzestuart58@gmail.com

Thanks

Like every book I've ever written, this one could not have seen the light of day without the help, ideas, suggestions, comments and support of a number of people:

Writing is a lonely occupation, but one learns early in one's writing career not to be "precious" about one's work, and to listen carefully to feedback and suggestions.

So first of all, my deepest thanks are to my wonderful wife Lorna who has gone through the manuscript of this book time and again and given me comment and criticism that kept me from straying from the central path.

While one can perhaps expect one's spouse and close family to engage in laborious assistance, it's another matter to impose on the kindness of others to do the same. I must give special thanks to

Stuart Jackson, whom I only met once, briefly, in an airport lounge, and who incredibly kindly agreed to read and give me feedback on an early draft. The feedback was invaluable. I can't thank you enough Stuart.

Great thanks also to Sarah Padfield who put an early draft of the book to the test of a university class at the University of Western Ontario in Canada. A trial by fire which, once again, provided excellent feedback.

And also huge thanks to George Campbell, Randy Findlay, Alejandro Serralde, Kevan Jones, Peter Smith, Peter Nixon, Tony Farugia, Richard Stagg, Alan Yu, Philip Johnston, Chris Dunn, and Rick Roskin for their insightful comments.

I know it sounds trite, but I couldn't have done it without you.

1

SECRET 1

Highly Effective Leadership is about influence, not position or authority

---

"If your actions inspire people to dream more, learn more, do more, you are a leader"

JOHN QUINCY ADAMS

The common belief is that leadership is essentially about authority, power and position. It isn't. **First of all, it's about influence.** The eminent psychologist, Dr Peter Honey, makes the point clearly: "Managers may have the right to command, but the commanded have the right to decide how far to obey".

Everything you do has an influence. Some of the things you do may exert more of an influence than others, but all of them have an impact. None have a zero effect.[7] An interesting way of thinking about influence is to see it as a service that people can buy or not buy. When the "service" is seen as having value, they buy into it, and when it's not, they don't.[8]

Daniel Goleman says, "Neuroscience has discovered that our brain's very design makes it sociable, inexorably drawn into an intimate brain-to-brain linkup whenever we engage with another person".[9] Whether you like it or not, what you do influences others, and others influence you, whoever they may be. By engaging with people, we influence them and influence equals leadership.

It's not about position. You can have a C-Suite title, you can tell people what you want them to do, and you can exert all your power and authority, but that doesn't necessarily mean they will do it. A four-year study of 286 organizations that fired their CEOs found that in more than half of the cases it was because the individual failed to "adequately sell the need to change". In other words, despite having position and authority, these individuals didn't have the most important thing - influence.[10]

In their book *Why Should Anyone Be Led by You?* Rob Goffee and Gareth Jones make the critically important point that, "the persistent misconception that people who occupy senior organizational positions are leaders has probably damaged our capacity to understand leadership more than anything else. It has blinded us to the true nature of leadership ... *Leaders at all levels make a difference to performance*" (italics ours).[11]

This myth about leaders only being people at the top of organizations is something that is repeated again and again in business magazines, papers and journals. The thinking is changing, but very slowly. Of *Fortune's* 2015 list of the world's top 50 leaders, all were people at the top of their organizations. In the 2017 list you could still count on the fingers of one hand individuals who didn't fit that description. In articles and books about leadership and leaders there is almost no mention of people in the middle of the organization and virtually none of the people at the bottom. For instance, in 2014 when the *Harvard Business Review* ran an article about the 100 best leaders, they were all CEOs.[12] In 2017 it featured an article, "The Best performing CEOs in the World, 2017".[13] In reality, it was a list of the best performing *companies* where CEOs had been in the role for more than two years. The conclusion we're meant to draw, of course, is that performance is a direct result of the magnificence of the CEO.

And Harvard Business School reinforces this idea: 62% of HBS cases feature standout, semi-heroic individuals who alone lead their organization to success.[14] Warren Bennis, the person *Forbes* magazine called "the dean of management gurus" said "One of the truly dreadful trends of the 1990s was the emergence of the celebrity CEO".[15]

What's so destructive about all of this is that it promotes the unstated but highly damaging conclusion that unless you're a major player, you're just a pawn in the game. That is painfully untrue. Leadership is about getting people to do things differently and making a difference, and that happens at all levels and in all functions of an organization.

Here's an example of someone at the bottom level of an organization, without any high-status job title, without any of the power and authority of position, but who got people to do things differently and made a major difference. Her name is Stacy Zimmer. Her job was to meet with everyone applying for access to a Regional Mental Health and Addictions Program, and to match them up with the most appropriate therapist. This involved dealing with a wide range of different clinicians and different functions, and a mountain of documentation. On her own initiative, to make the process more efficient, she drove the move to a new documentation system that includes all inpatients, outpatients and the main regional hospital partner. Without position or authority, she got buy-in from doctors, therapists, managers and individuals in various departments, all

ROBIN STUART-KOTZE

of whom changed their approach. The result was a process that is more effective, more clinician- and client-friendly, and which allows clinicians to spend more time with their clients.

How do you exert influence?

People form impressions and make judgements about you within the first 11 milliseconds of seeing you.[16] How you present your-self – your behaviour - influences others positively or negatively. Researchers Nalini Rambady and Robert Rosenthal say, "The way in which people move, talk and gesture – their facial expressions, posture and speech – all contribute to the formation of impressions about them". Their studies show that observation of as little as 30 seconds of behaviour results in judgements that are as accurate as five minutes of observation.[17]

In terms of leading and leadership it's not only vital to recognize the importance of first impressions, it's also helpful to understand what sustains that impression, and perhaps what you can do about it.[18] The problem is that once people have formed an impression, they discount things that run counter to their opinion. In addition, they act in ways that help to prove their initial opinion correct.[19] It's about not wanting to admit to themselves that they might be wrong.

What can you do to manage the impression others have of you? If you can pick up clues from their actions and act in ways that either reinforce their favourable impression, or act differently from what they expect if their initial impression is unfavourable, you can help things go your way. One if the most powerful influencing forces is similarity – you are attracted to people who bear some similarity to you, and vice-versa. The similarity may be in things like background (same school, same city, military service), similar opinions, similar life-style, same age, religion, sports interests,

16

or dress.[20] Even pointing out small similarities, for instance "My mother was also from (country)", influences positive responses from others. If you want to reinforce a favourable impression or counter an unfavourable one, first of all try to focus on what makes you, in some way, similar to the other person.

Another way to use the issue of similarity is to show that a lot of people act like you. When a large number of people act similarly, dress similarly, speak similarly, etc., it becomes increasingly difficult to resist the pressure to disagree. The classic experiment demonstrating the power of social comparison was done by Solomon Asch.[21] It involved eight individuals, only one of whom was the actual subject of the experiment. The other seven were confederates of Asch's. The experiment involved viewing the length of lines on a screen and deciding whether one was either longer or shorter than the comparison line. In the experiment, one after another, the confederates gave their responses first, before the subject was asked for a response. The subject always answered last. At certain times the confederates were instructed to all give an incorrect answer. Even when the difference in the two lines being compared was obvious, subjects agreed with the incorrect answer more than a third of the time.

Emotional contagion

Shakespeare said, "There are more things in Heaven and Earth than are dreamt of". And in terms of the human brain he was right: there are infinitely more things that occur in the subconscious brain than are noticed consciously. One of these processes is what is known as *emotional contagion*.[22][23] It's not just your actions that get noticed, it's the emotions that you express with those actions. Marketing research showed that when an individual smiled, another person, simply seeing the smile, would have a positive attitude to a product which they were considering.[24]

Emotional contagion works both ways, affecting negative as well as positive feelings and attitudes. A research study looked at the effect of leaders' use of favouritism toward certain employees. Employees witnessing the behaviour developed negative emotions about the leader, and emotional contagion spread these feelings down through the organization, resulting in what the researchers described as "organizational-level disapproval of the leader and cynicism towards the leader".[25]

The brain processes what we see two ways, one of which we can very loosely describe as happening at a conscious level where the information flows from the eyes to the thalamus and then to the visual cortex. But there is another process which occurs where the information goes directly from the thalamus to the amygdala. That's the ancient part of the brain that interprets what we see and triggers the fight, flight, submission reaction. It picks up the tiniest clues from people's expressions, posture and movements and, at a subconscious level, dictates our reaction to them. Most of the time we are completely unaware of these reactions.

Research into the effect of more than two hundred behaviour traits shows that two things – warmth and competence – account for more than 90% of the impression, positive or negative, that people have of you.[26] But note, it's warmth *and* competence. You need to exhibit both, although warmth takes precedence. Lead with that because the brain picks up on warmth faster than competence.[27] And research shows that when you smile, along with projecting warmth, you are perceived to be more competent.[28]

Mirroring

We think we communicate with others by what we say and by our overt actions, but we don't know the half of it. In face-to-face situations, we communicate through a very subtle form of behaviour known as *mirroring*. When we recognize the expression of an emotion – a smile, a frown, a narrowing of the eyes, a slight downturn of the mouth – even though these expressions may be minute and fleeting, our own facial muscles move to mirror what we see. This happens even when we don't realise it consciously.

By mirroring we create an emotional connection with the other party, either reinforcing positive emotions or negative ones. So, when you approach an encounter with a service provider, if you do so in a pleasant frame of mind, (remember, warmth is a major factor in creating a positive impression) a slight, unconscious friendly gesture of yours will send a message and the service provider will tend to mirror it. That will start things off in the right direction. If you then reinforce that with a smile, ask for assistance or advice, and thirdly say thanks, you will have raised the probability of a positive experience a hundred times. [29]

As an aside, the sad fact is that 14% of people smile less than five times a day.[30] "So what?", you say. You're not always trying to get good service from people, so why do you have to smile a lot? It depends whether or not you'd like to live a long time. Smiling is positively correlated with longevity – the more you smile the greater your chances of living longer.[31] It's not difficult to find things that make you smile. Simply looking at a picture of a happy face or an emoji of a happy face causes the muscles around your mouth to, at least momentarily, contract upwards in a smile.[32]

An interesting sidelight to this phenomenon of mirroring is the effect of pharmaceutical or surgical techniques such as botox injections that alter movement and expression in an individual's face. These mask the person's emotions so that we can't read them as clearly as we might, and as a result we don't develop the same degree of empathy with them.

What's happening here is that because we can't read their emotional signals properly, we can't mirror them properly. We don't understand what they're feeling or communicating. But making the interaction even more difficult, *they* can't read *us* because we aren't mirroring what they think they're feeling. Because the individual's facial inflexibility makes it more difficult for them to mirror what they are seeing in our face, we see them as less likeable. The mirroring is confused, and the brain says you can't trust what you can't read.

Dominance vs. earned prestige as influence

If you ask people how influence is exerted the answer tends to come back as things like by exerting your authority, by persuasion, by logical explanation, by offering an incentive reward, and so on – carrot and stick. The common element in all these actions is that you're the central character in the piece. *You* offer the carrot and *you* threaten with the stick. Everything comes from *your* perspective, *your* view, *your* wants, and *your* assumptions, and it makes no effort to listen to or understand the other person. It's dominance: you place yourself in the position of controller, with results being completely due to your actions.

Research indicates that there are some unexpected consequences of relying on dominance to exert influence. The more dominance and power you display, the less power the people you're dealing with have. It's a zero-sum game. The greater the gap between your perceived power and theirs, the more reluctant people are to make suggestions or share ideas. The research suggests that the other side of the coin is influence that is derived from earned prestige. You earn prestige by being competent and reliable, but you *multiply* that in the eyes of others by showing them respect, and asking for their ideas, and giving them recognition.[33]

The euphemism for that type of behaviour is "political skill", and a study of 35 school administrators and 474 branch managers of a service firm showed that people who were more "politically skilled" (defined as "the ability to effectively understand others at work, and to use such knowledge to influence others to act in ways that enhance one's personal and/or organizational objectives") were rated as being more effective as leaders and were seen as better performers.[34]

The effectiveness of Ask Them (AT) behaviour vs. Tell Them (TT) behaviour in influencing behaviour

Adam Grant talks about "powerless communication" and how it is highly effective in building prestige and influence.[35] Its principles run counter to what we might think are ways to influence people, but hard research data shows them to be correct. It's about asking questions rather than telling people "the answers", asking people for their thoughts, ideas and advice rather than giving them solutions, admitting to weaknesses rather than just trumpeting strengths, talking tentatively rather than laying down the law, and so on.

In our book, *Performance*, we talked about and demonstrated the benefits of using an Ask Them (*AT*) approach to leadership rather than a Tell Them (*TT*) approach.[36] *AT* results in high-level performance, and the reason it does is that it engages the energy, experience, creativity, ideas and suggestions of every individual in the organization, top to bottom. Here are some examples.

In an obituary in *The Times* for Major John Sim, MC, a second world war army officer who inspired and influenced his men to extraordinary levels of courage and accomplishment, one of his soldiers described his leadership as "He guided and looked after you, but never over-supervised you; he let you *do* things".[37]

A great example of the power of asking people rather than telling them is Mark Parker, CEO of Nike (and *Fortune*'s 2015 Business Person of the Year). Under Parker, Nike's revenues doubled from $15 billion to $31 billion, and profits reached $3.1 billion in 2015. One of the outstanding leadership characteristics he displays is asking questions of his people that get *them* to find the solutions and to deliver them. Parker describes his management style as being like an editor, focusing on helping people develop their ideas.

Google is an *AT* company. Prasad Setty, Vice President of People Analytics and Compensation, says "we think that if we give people freedom, they will amaze us".[38] Google solicits and uses feedback from employees on everything from how they would like to be compensated to the design of the company bicycles.

Southwest Airlines is another *AT* company. It conducts twice yearly surveys to get candid feedback from employees across the company and listens to what they say. Its stock price has increased by 120% in the ten years between 2006 and 2016 and it has the highest customer satisfaction of the nine major US airlines.

Hyatt Hotels encourages and supports its people to listen to guests and to discover their preferences, likes and complaints. They are empowered to act on this information and make guests feel special. Hyatt has the lowest staff turnover of any major hotel chain.

Every employee of the John Lewis Partnership – all 76,000+ of them – is a partner and owner of the retailer and supermarket chain.[39] There is a mechanism for employees' suggestions and complaints to get to the board, and a weekly staff magazine where people can express their opinions, anonymously, about any company issue. Revenue has grown steadily, year on year, for the past ten years.

Perhaps the biggest reason why people withhold their ideas, suggestions, observations and concerns is that they don't think management will do anything about them.[40] So for instance if you ask people to respond to a survey about some issues, make sure you do two things: provide them with the results of the survey, no matter how negative they may appear, and secondly let them know what actions you're going to take to address the issues.

When you show people that you actually listen to them and that you respect them and their ideas, you create a sense of community where they recognize that they can all be helpful to each other and all respect each other. Research confirms that this behaviour gets people to share knowledge, work together, and help one another.[41] On the other hand, if people don't believe you're listening, they're far less likely to share ideas and suggestions.[42] And they're more likely to become emotionally exhausted, and to quit.[43]

The positive results of asking for advice or help

Here's an interesting fact which begins to explain why an Ask Them approach works well. If you ask someone for their advice or help, they don't just give it and move on, *they feel a responsibility for the success of their advice and they will work to help you achieve it.* It's not necessarily because they particularly want you to succeed; they don't want their advice to be a failure. And they feel good about being asked because it makes them feel valued and important.

Research also shows that individuals who make a habit of asking for advice or help from knowledgeable others receive higher performance evaluations than those who never do.[44] Part of the reason for this has to do with the fact that these individuals tend to have a better record of problem solving, and that's because when you explain a problem you're having and ask someone for their advice, they need to look at the problem from *your* point of view. They need to, at least to some extent, place themselves in your shoes, and they become more committed to helping find a solution. Adam Grant says, "Seeking advice is a subtle way to invite someone to make a commitment to us".[45]

An *AT* approach provides those that are asked with a sense of control and choice, a sense of involvement, and a sense of self-respect.[46] Charles Duhigg, *New York Times* business reporter and author of the best-seller, *The Power of Habit*, comments that "Simply giving employees a sense of agency – a feeling that they are in control, that they have genuine decision-making authority – can radically increase how much energy and focus they bring to their jobs".[47]

Frank Flynn studied engineers at a big telecoms firm, and looked at them in terms of what Adam Grant calls givers, takers or matchers.[48] In simple terms, givers are focused on what other people need from them, takers are focused on what they can get from other people, and matchers try to attain a balance between giving and taking. What Flynn found was that the most productive engineers gave more often and gave more than they received. Not only did they have the highest level of productivity, but they were also the most admired by their peers. By both giving help to others, and asking for and getting help from them, these engineers built strong bonds of trust among their peers and were given help even by those to whom they hadn't given any.

Building the two-way street

We underestimate the degree to which people find asking for help embarrassing.[49] So if you reverse things and put yourself in the position where you see someone struggling and you would like them to come to you for advice or help, you need to recognize how hard it is for them to do that. The way to get around the problem is to pre-empt the issue by *you* asking *them* for some help or advice on an issue. That pushes the defensive screens aside. You've just overcome a huge artificial, but never the less quite real, barrier to communication and engagement because you've shown respect for them and their ideas.

Guess who feels good about that? Everyone wants to feel valued. If you know you're valued, you feel good about yourself. If you feel you're seen as worthless, it's the absolute opposite. Being made to feel worthless creates anger and resentment, and this tends to make people actively disengaged – hostile and destructive.

There's also another element at play here that supports the fact that people are more willing to give help than we believe. Research shows that people experience a psychological "cost" for refusing a request for help. When they're asked for help or assistance they feel that there is a "cost for saying no".[50]

Also, people respond much more positively to a request for help that is made in terms of a state of need than when the appeal is made in terms of it being their duty or responsibility to give the help.[51] When you ask people for their views, suggestions or help, you have to be genuine about it and you have to listen and respond appropriately.[52] People don't like being taken for suckers and they watch carefully to see if what they offer is taken seriously.

Reciprocation

Perhaps the most powerful influencing factor is reciprocation. Robert Cialdini, a leading figure in the field of influence, says that in terms of influencing people, they will help you if they owe you for something you did to help them, even if it was very minor.[53] The more you exchange favours with others, the more your performance improves. Creating a sense of reciprocity makes all parties feel like winners.

We have an underlying, compelling need to reciprocate for any gift or favour we receive. If someone does you a favour you feel you should return the favour; if someone gives you a gift you feel you should give them a gift in return, and so on. If you think this occurs only when the person likes you but not when they don't, you would be wrong. The fact is that simply doing something for someone hugely increases the likelihood of them doing you a favour in return, whether they like you or not.[54] The reason is that the act of reciprocation provides them with a good feeling about themselves – they like themselves more. The proof that it's this positive feeling that generates the behaviour is demonstrated by the fact that when a giver refuses to accept a reciprocal gift or favour of any kind, he or she is disliked.[55] The giver has prevented you from feeling good about yourself by being able to give back.

Consistency

People attempt to achieve consistency between their actions and their beliefs. For instance, you need to buy a car and there are a number of choices which create some level of uncertainty in the decision. However, once you make the decision you work to convince yourself that you made the *right* decision and you behave consistently with that. You tell others about the car's good features, recommend it, etc. In other words, you work to reduce the dissonance between your action to buy the car and your belief about whether it was the best buy. The principle was graphically illustrated by research done with people betting at a racetrack.[56] Bettors about to make a bet stated they felt the horse had "a fair chance of winning". But after having made the bet they said they believed it had "a *good* chance of winning". They needed to reinforce to themselves that their decision was right, so they acted consistently with that.

There is a strong need in people to behave, and appear to behave, consistently with their view of themselves. If you see yourself as a conscientious person, then you are more likely to do the best job you can when asked. If you see yourself as an active person, then you're more likely to engage in various types of activities. The same is true for others. You just have to get them to see themselves that way. If, for instance, when someone gives you something or does something for you, you say "Thank you; you're a kind and thoughtful person", they begin to think of themselves that way and tend to act that way. Which leads us to the next issue, priming.

Priming

The concept of priming is that exposure to one stimulus influences how you experience a second stimulus. In other words, what you present first to someone affects how they perceive what you present to them next. This is a very important point so it's worth repeating: *what you present first to someone affects how they perceive what you present to them next.*

For example, people act quietly when they enter a library.[57] Being shown pictures of certain types of guns primes aggressive thoughts.[58] People who wear fake luxury sunglasses tend to cheat more.[59] Where people vote affects how they vote.[60] Holding a hot cup of coffee makes you feel more positive about someone; holding an iced drink has the opposite effect.[61] Larger numbers have a different effect than smaller numbers. When people were asked how much they'd spend on dinner in two restaurants, "Studio 17" or "Studio 97", they said they'd pay more in Studio 97.[62]

It's not accidental that judges in a courtroom sit at an elevated level above the rest of the court. That's telling you who has power and requires respectful behaviour. It primes the behaviour of the others in the court to show respect. Organizational life is full of these priming cues. The higher the rank an individual has in an organization the larger their workspace, and quite often the higher the floor level on which they work.[63]

The distance between the entrance to an office and where its incumbent sits is a subtle priming clue as to how to behave in relation to that person. There's a story about when Hitler went to Italy during World War II to meet Mussolini that shows that both of them understood the effects of priming. Mussolini sat at the far end of a very long room and when Hitler entered he walked halfway towards Mussolini and stopped so that Mussolini had to walk the other half length of the room to meet him.

Compliments

We'll talk more about compliments in a later chapter when we look at motivation. What makes them powerful influencers is that they are a form of positive recognition and we all appreciate being told something complimentary about ourselves – good work, great idea, smart jacket, etc. – even, it appears, when the compliment is not deserved and clearly untrue.[64] Nor can flattery be overdone. Contrary to popular belief that it only works up to a point and then, when it's overdone, has an opposite result, there appears to be no limit to the amount of flattery people accept and like. And it gets even more surreal. Flattery from a computer produces the same effect as flattery from a human.[65]

Involvement

A key element in influencing people is to involve them and to make them part of the solution, not part of the problem. Everyone wants to feel they are recognized as having some value. Interestingly, research shows you don't even have to be the person initiating the recognition. You can enable people to feel recognized by getting *them* to identify how they add value.[66]

In a health care organization, employees were invited to create new, fun titles for their jobs. Examples were an x-ray technician retitling the job "bone seeker", an infectious disease specialist becoming a "germ slayer", and so on. Results showed that people felt more recognized for their work, were less emotionally exhausted, and felt abler to talk about and share information. In another company, groups of employees doing similar jobs were asked to create a common job title for themselves. Job satisfaction rose 16% and the employees identified more strongly with the company.

A worldwide study, reported by *Forbes*, surveyed 30,000 employees and found that upwards of 50% wanted to leave their jobs.[67] The major thing that people don't like about their jobs, is how they are led. Another survey found that 35% of people would be willing to forego "a substantial pay raise" in return for having their boss fired.[68] Bill Clinton famously said, "it's the economy, stupid". In this case, substitute the word "leadership" for the word "economy".

Key points from the chapter

- Leadership is, first of all, about influence

- Everything you do or say – including things you do unconsciously – has an impact

- You don't have to have a position or title of authority to be a leader; people at all levels can make a difference

- People form impressions and make judgements about you within the first 11 milliseconds of seeing you

- Once people have formed an impression, they discount things that run counter to that, and secondly, they act in ways that help to prove their initial opinion correct

- If you want to reinforce a favourable impression or counter an unfavourable one, try to focus on what makes you, in some way, similar to the other person

- Two things – warmth and competence – account for more than 90% of the impression, positive or negative, that people have of you

- Lead with warmth because the brain picks up on warmth faster than competence

- When you smile, along with projecting warmth, you are perceived to be more competent

- You don't just communicate through words and actions; your emotions are picked up and have an effect on others

- Asking can be more powerful than telling because it gets the involvement of others.

- If you ask someone for their advice or help, they don't just give it and move on, they feel a responsibility for the success of their advice and they will work to help you achieve it

- Individuals who make a habit of asking for advice or help from knowledgeable others receive higher performance evaluations than those who never do so

- One of the most powerful influencing factors is reciprocation

- We like people who are similar to us. The similarity may be in a wide range of things like background, opinions, life-style, age, religion, sports interests, and even dress

- There is a strong need in people to behave, and appear to behave, consistently with their view of themselves

- What you present first to someone affects how they perceive what you present to them next – the priming effect

- A key element in influencing people is to involve them and to make them part of the solution, not part of the problem

2

SECRET 2

Highly Effective Leadership is about behaviour, not personality

---

"As far as other people are concerned, you are your behaviour"

DR PETER HONEY

Leadership is about behaviour. It's about what you *do* – your actions and your decisions. You influence things by what you do, not what you think or hope. People *see* your actions; they don't see your thoughts or wishes.

Every action has a consequence. Every decision has an impact and aftermath. Newton's Third Law, true of physical forces, states that for every action there is an equal and opposite reaction. A reaction to a decision or an action may not be "equal and opposite" but there is always a reaction. One of the reasons we tend to get into trouble is that we don't adequately think through the connection between action and consequence. Failing to understand this connection is amusingly recognized by the Darwin Awards. One of our favourite

Darwin Award winners is the terrorist who mailed a lethal letter bomb with insufficient postage and when it was returned, opened it.

Of course what you say has influence, but people watch to see if you follow the words with actions. People pay much more attention to, and are more influenced by, what you *do* rather than what you say. It's worthwhile following the advice of the early 20ᵗʰ century industrialist, Andrew Carnegie, who said, "As I grow older I pay less attention to what people say. I just watch what they do".

There is an interesting piece of research which shows that what you do as a leader has far greater power than what you say.[69] Young children were presented with a game situation where they watched adults perform a task and either reward themselves only for good performance, or also reward themselves when their performance was poor. After watching the adult's behaviour, the children also played the game.

Three situations were tested: (1) where the adult only rewarded herself for good performance, and only rewarded the children for good performance, (2) where the adult only rewarded herself for good performance but gave rewards to the children regardless of their performance, and (3) where the adult rewarded herself for poor performance, but didn't do so for the children.

When left to play alone, in the second situation where the children's' performance had been treated leniently, they remained lenient on themselves. In the third situation where the children were held to a stringent level of performance, but the adult was lenient with herself, half of them subsequently adopted the same leniency towards themselves and half maintained the stringent performance levels of the adult model. But *without exception*, all the children in the first situation, where they had learned from a tough-on-herself model who was equally stringent on them, adopted the same stringent standard of performance for themselves. Do as I do, rather than Do as I say, has a highly influential effect. And this effect is magnified further when the role model is perceived to be powerful.[70]

It's a leader's behaviour that makes a difference

Fortune describes the old General Motors culture as one where "people try hard not to bring bad news to higher-ups... Practically no one is ever held accountable for a decision, partly because most decisions are made by committees, and even then, the process is a charade because key participants agree privately on the outcome ahead of time... rare threats to the established order can almost always be waited out." [71]

The recognition that behaviour – what one does rather than what one says – is what makes a difference is illustrated by how Mary Barra, the CEO of General Motors, is changing the culture of the company. Barra says, "culture is how people behave", and so she says that the way she plans to change that culture is, "by behaving differently every day than any GM CEO has behaved in decades ... it's (about) changing behaviours."[72]

Behaviour sends a message, and in the wake of the findings of the Valukas report into the faults of GM's Cobalt car, Mary Barra took two early actions that sent the very clear message that the old culture was dead: she fired 15 people and moved seven high-level executives. She expects different behaviour from her top team – directness, transparency and candour – and she says "I'm not asking people to do it. It's a requirement – not only that they hold themselves accountable to do it, but they hold each other accountable. That's the message I've delivered and will continue to drive through the whole organization. This is not optional."

But behaviour isn't just important in large organizations, it's critical in every type of venture. Research with 1,088 entrepreneurs found that the action of making a written business plan increased the probability of success by 16%.[73] That may not sound like much, but anything that improves the chances of success for a start-up is worth attention.

How a leader behaves has a huge impact on performance. Research in a technology services company that rotated group supervisors every few months so that workers would have different bosses showed that replacing a boss who was ranked in the bottom ten% in terms of effectiveness with a boss ranked in the top ten% produced the equivalent in output of adding one more person to the group.[74]

Non-verbal behaviour

A lot, in fact the majority, of the things you do are subconscious. But while you may not be aware of them, they're picked up by others, also to a large extent subconsciously. This is what's called non-verbal communication. You communicate messages non-verbally with things like facial expression, body movement, and posture. You also do it through things like the tone of your voice, your choice of words, and the different emphasis you put on words.

Non-verbal behaviour has a much stronger effect in communication than words, either spoken and written. Non-verbal cues have more than four times the effect of spoken words.[75] For instance, making direct eye contact, rather than not looking directly at someone causes them to rate you higher on credibility.[76] Facial expressiveness of public speakers makes them more persuasive, and their audience rates them higher in competence.[77]

Can you learn how to be a leader?

The answer is "Yes". Leaders are made, not born, and that's confirmed by research.[78] Anyone who tells you differently has some
sort of agenda.

It's not your genes that determine what you do. Yes, you have about
24,000 genes which you got from birth, and yes, genes don't change.
But the way they work does change.[79] Genes create proteins and
these proteins control functions of the brain and body that in turn
affect behaviour. Things you experience turn the gene creation
of proteins on or off so that you feel and act differently.[80] The
behaviour of people around you (social behaviour) affects gene
readout to the brain and that affects the way you act.[81][82] It also
affects things like your immune system. When you go through
a stressful experience you are more susceptible to illness.[83]

Everyone can change their behaviour. Don't fall for that line that it's
your personality or your genes that determine what and who you
are. That's nonsense. You *aren't* held captive by genetics. Your level
of knowledge, intelligence and skill set is *not* fixed. Life is made
up of experiences. Everyone can learn, and everyone can become
better at things. What you learn changes how you act and react.

You learn best by doing. It's largely a process of trial and error
that you go through over the length of your life. As a small child
you learn that touching something that is very hot is painful and
you try not to do it again. As you grow up you find that when you
help someone they tend to return the gesture. It's about cause
and effect. And, most importantly, you can also learn from the
experience of others. That's the principal reason why the Harvard
Business School and others teach by the case method; you get to
experience and learn vicariously through other people's successful
or unsuccessful actions and decisions.

An organization that you may not have heard of, and that *The Economist* called "Headless" is an excellent example of how people learn to be leaders.[84] It is the Orpheus Chamber Orchestra in New York. The orchestra doesn't have a conductor. It calls itself a multi-leader organization where leadership of various sections, let alone the whole orchestra, is rotated among its members, and where members also take on tasks such as designing their programmes, selecting the music, managing public relations, raising funds for the orchestra, etc. It's a great example of the fact that *the best way to develop leaders is to give people leadership responsibility.* Leadership training is an abstract; leading is a reality.

A number of things happen when people are given leadership responsibility. They learn how to speak up about things, to initiate actions without being told to or being asked to, and they learn how to communicate with others, work with them, and to get other people to cooperate with them. Because they have responsibility for the success of what they're doing, they become engaged.

They also learn something which is invaluable for successful leadership, but which many people find difficult or uncomfortable. They learn to ask for feedback from others and to pay attention to it. It's a truism that you can't improve at doing something unless you know what you're doing currently. But because we are all self-centred to one degree or other, our vision of what we're doing tends to be biased and clouded.

As the great Scottish bard, Robbie Burns, so nicely put it, (and we ask forgiveness from his admirers for "translating" his words from the Scottish dialect of his day to our highly unpoetic everyday language) "If we could be given the gift to see ourselves as others see us, it would free us from making many mistakes".[85]

People think they listen, but generally they do so selectively. Listening actively – not just to the words being spoken, but to the way they're expressed, the tone, the context, the underlying emotion, the body language involved – requires effort and control of one's own emotions, but it's a key to effective leadership.

Is practice the key?

There's a very old joke about a visitor to New York stopping a person on the street and asking how to get to Carnegie Hall, to which the reply is "Practice, practice, practice". Malcolm Gladwell, in his book *Outliers*, claimed that mastery of a field of endeavour required 10,000 hours of deliberate practice. So if you spend 10,000 hours learning to be a successful leader will you become one? Ten thousand hours amounts to somewhere in the range of four to five years of work, depending on how many hours a day you work. However, if it was simply an issue of time spent to master something, why don't the millions of people who practice their swing at golf ranges become excellent golfers, or the millions of people around the world who practice and play soccer become top league players? Part of the answer is that they aren't practicing the right things. Unless you hit a golf ball in precisely the right manner with precisely the right swing you aren't going to hit it well. So, for starters, you have to have the *right* kind of practice.

However, another much more important part of the answer is that it depends on the skill or knowledge being learned. Research at Princeton University analysed the results of 88 studies of deliberate practice and found that while practice explained 26% of the variance in games performance, and 18% of the variance in sports performance, it only explained 1% of performance in professions – i.e. business and organizational life.[86]

The more something is governed by stable rules and structures – for example chess and classical music – the more people are able to master the required skills and actions through practice. But when it comes to life in organizations it becomes *far* more complicated because jobs change all the time, conditions change, expectations change, technology changes, and so on. In that sort of environment, practicing becoming an expert at doing something specific isn't much use when that something is no longer part of the job.

The effect of leadership behaviours

Working with, observing, and talking with several tens of thousands of leaders at every level in organizations, we discovered that different behaviours have different effects on performance. Before you say, "If I've ever heard a blatant statement of the obvious, this one takes the prize", let us explain a bit further. What we discovered when we talked with people was that the actions they take do one of three things: they *accelerate* performance, they *sustain* performance, or they *hinder* performance.

Performance accelerating behaviour is centred on actions that drive changes and improvements, create vision and direction, generate excitement and commitment, take the offensive against competitors, inspire a winning culture, ensure that systems and processes operate optimally, increase returns, and improve effectiveness. The behaviour's focus is on adding value by doing things differently and better. It constantly questions existing systems, existing structures, existing assumptions, and existing ways of operating. Performance accelerating behaviour is managing the changing, the unknown, and the unpredictable. It requires vision and the ability to get people to go where they have not countenanced going before. It is leadership behaviour that is focused on changing things, and doing things differently. It is about making a difference and challenging the status quo.

Performance sustaining leadership behaviour is about making sure operations, systems and procedures work smoothly. It's about quality, efficiency and consistency, and about maintaining stakeholder value. It is focused on actions that produce reliable results, maintain efficiency, deliver projects and products on budget and on time, and provide people with the necessary skills and abilities to perform their jobs well. It preserves knowledge and skills and ensures processes and procedures are implemented and followed.

Performance acceleration gets the glamour because changes are exciting. Accelerating performance is one thing, but sustaining it is equally important. To use a military analogy, you can't move an army, successively engaging the enemy, without support systems and processes. Napoleon generally gets the credit, but it was actually Frederick the Great who said, "An army marches on its stomach". It's no use being able to make the very best widget in the world at the very best price if you can't deliver it and get paid for it, or if its quality isn't consistent.

Sustaining actions make sure things run as they should, that products get delivered on time, that payment is collected on time, that quality is maintained, that regulations are complied with, and so on. No organization can survive without a significant degree of performance sustaining behaviour. All the outwardly glamorous and exciting businesses of the world like investment banking, advertising, motion pictures, fashion design, etc., have "back office" teams that manage all the processes and administrative bits and pieces, that get the financial deals completed, the media campaigns distributed, and the fashion shows presented.

Research demonstrates how important performance sustaining behaviour is to the success of a company. In a recent article in the *Harvard Business Review*, Michael Mankins and Richard Steele summarised a study done in 2004 in collaboration with *The Economist Intelligence Unit* in which they surveyed senior executives from 197 companies worldwide with sales in excess of $500 million, exploring how successfully their corporations were at translating strategy into performance. The findings were highly revealing. They found that on average almost 30% of performance was lost due to inadequate levels of performance sustaining behaviour.[87]

The balance of behaviour

Effective leadership requires a balance between performance accelerating behaviour and performance sustaining behaviour. Using the analogy of a car, there is a balance that must be achieved between accelerating and sustaining movement. You can't accelerate indefinitely because that will simply spin the car out of control. And there are various systems in the car that must be kept performing properly – the fuel feed, the valves and pistons, the transmission, the steering mechanism, the suspension, the brakes, etc. These are essential to maintain the car's movement. The accelerator is only applied when it's necessary to go faster. The same is true of organizations. Competitive pressures, technological developments and customer demands require that the organization constantly improve performance in certain areas. But at the same time consistency must be maintained in the management of inventories, supply chains, receivables, staffing, quality, and a host of other things.

Can an organization have too much performance accelerating behaviour? The answer is yes, and here's an example. The president of a technology company we know lost his job, not because he wasn't an inspirational leader or because he didn't surround himself with people who subscribed to a common vision and drove change forward, but because he didn't make sure the company had enough people focusing on performance sustaining behaviour. His behaviour was focused very strongly on accelerating performance, and so was the behaviour of his team and the teams below them. They were a darling of the markets – until they reported incorrect figures for the company's performance not once but three times in short succession. The market overlooked the first mistake because it was quickly dealt with, very grudgingly forgave the second, but lost its patience at the third.

On the other hand, too great a focus on performance sustaining behaviour and not enough on performance accelerating results in complacency and stagnation. An FMCG company that failed to adapt its products to changing consumer preferences became bogged down in process, failed to implement new technology, and failed to improve productivity. It experienced a dramatic fall in revenue and market share and saw its market value plummet by over 50% in the space of 12 months. Its inability to put adequate emphasis on performance accelerating behaviour led to its being taken over by a competitor and almost all its management being let go.

Balance of behaviour is critically important. The most difficult task for any leader, at any level, and in any job, is to get the balance right. Individuals and organizations that ignore this do so at their peril. Too much performance accelerating leadership behaviour and not enough performance sustaining behaviour results in loss of control and confusion. Too much performance sustaining behaviour and not enough performance accelerating behaviour results in complacency and stagnation. We will talk about the third type of behaviour, performance hindering, in chapter 8.

Key points from this chapter

- Leadership is about what you *do* – your actions and your decisions; people *see* your actions; they don't see your thoughts or wishes

- What you do as a leader has far greater power than what you say

- Non-verbal behaviour has a much stronger effect in communication than words, either spoken and written. Non-verbal cues have more than four times the effect of spoken words

- Leaders are made, not born, and that's confirmed by research

- The effectiveness of leaders' behaviour is determined by the situations in which they find themselves

- The things you do as a leader either accelerate performance, sustain performance, or hinder performance

- Performance accelerating behaviour is focused on changing things, and doing things differently

- Performance sustaining behaviour is about making sure operations, systems and procedures work smoothly – about quality, efficiency and consistency

- Effective leadership requires a balance between performance accelerating behaviour and performance sustaining behaviour

3

So why isn't Effective Leadership about personality?

Effective leadership isn't about personality because personality only predicts 10-15% of behaviour. [88] [89] Effective leadership is about what you do, not who or what you are.

However, the myth that personality predicts performance and success is very much alive and well. A recent *Wall Street Journal* article made the claim that introverts make great entrepreneurs. [90] To support this argument the article listed six examples of intro-verted entrepreneurs – Bill Gates, Steve Wozniak, Larry Page, Mark Zuckerberg, Marissa Mayer, and Warren Buffett. But any scientist will tell you that you cannot generalise from the particular. Because these specific six successful entrepreneurs may be introverted does not mean that *all* successful entrepreneurs are introverted. That's like saying that because Roger Federer and Stan Wawrinka are Swiss, all Swiss men are great tennis players.

We could quite easily make precisely the opposite argument that *extroverts* make great entrepreneurs because the following people are extroverts: Elon Musk, Richard Branson, Hasso Plattner, Alan Sugar, and Michael O'Leary. We probably don't have to tell you who Musk or Branson are because they have become virtual brand names. But in case you aren't familiar with Hasso Plattner, he's the billionaire co-founder and chairman of SAP, the German business software company that dominates the industry. Plattner is described as a "red-meat-for-breakfast" person with an "out-there personality". Lord Sugar is the billionaire entrepreneur who built his businesses from nothing and hosts the UK version of *The Apprentice*. Michael O'Leary built the largest airline in Europe, Ryanair, the first airline to carry 10,000,000 passengers a month. Saying he is outspoken and extroverted is a big understatement.

One of the problems with personality is that people use the word in everyday language quite differently from the way that a behavioural scientist uses it. People talk about individuals as having a *nice* personality, a *cheerful* personality, an *unpleasant* personality, *lots of* personality, or even *no* personality. The lyrics to a late 50's song describe how a person "walks with personality, talks with personality, smiles with personality, charms with personality and loves with personality".[91]

When people talk about someone having a type of personality, what they're doing is trying to provide a prediction of how we can expect this individual to act across a variety of situations. Sometimes the person may act in the way predicted, and sometimes not. The neuroscientist Dr Dean Burnett puts it quite clearly: "Nobody behaves the same way in all contexts; the external situation matters".[92]

Please re-read that last sentence. It's the key reason why personality doesn't predict behaviour or performance.

Research shows that the principal factor determining people's behaviour is the situation in which they find themselves, and that their behaviour changes as the situation changes.[93] [94]

An example of behaviour changing due to a change in the situation is someone who is rude and inconsiderate to those who have little power, but polite, engaging and even obsequious to those who are more powerful or of higher status. Or if you don't like that example, how about the fact that even noisy people tend to become quieter when they enter a place of religious worship. Or that they act very differently in stores when there are Black Friday sales.

The Oxford dictionary's rather circular definition of personality illustrates much of the problem of grasping what it is. It defines it as: "the combination of characteristics or qualities that form an individual's distinctive character". The key word here is "characteristic", in the sense of being typical. If we say something is characteristic of an individual, we imply that she or he demonstrates it most of the time. But we've just shown that is not necessarily the case.

The idea of personality is attractive because, as Stephen Covey says, "The glitter of the Personality Ethic, the massive appeal, is that there is some quick and easy way to achieve quality of life ... without going through the natural process of work and growth that makes it possible".[95]

And don't believe what personality tests tell you. *Research shows that 75% of people get a different result when they do a personality test again.*[96] So if you've done a personality test, should you do another, or another? Which result are you going to believe?

Descriptions of personality types are excellent subjects for what psychologists term "projection": that is projecting one's feelings, beliefs, attitudes, etc. onto something. The classic experiment that proved that this is exactly what happens was conducted by Bertram Forer.[97] He gave a group of individuals a personality test and then handed them back their results – ostensibly they were the results from the test, but in fact they were randomised astrological forecasts from a book he had bought at a nearby newsstand. When he asked the individuals how accurate, on a scale of 0 (poor) to 5 (perfect), they found their profiles, 40% gave a perfect 5 and the average score for the group was 4.2.

Personality is preference

Personality is best understood as how a person *prefers* to behave, given no constraints. The key phrase here is *given no constraints*. If you'd prefer to be rude and bullying to people ("that's my personality"), and if the situation allows you to indulge that preference, you'll do so. But if it doesn't, you won't.

One of the main reasons that personality explains so little of behaviour is that life is not without constraints. We talk about spoilt children and their behaviour. What makes them "spoilt" is their parents' pandering to their every preference – i.e. placing no constraints on their behaviour. As an infant or young child, given no constraints, the tendency is towards self-gratification with little or no concern for others. You want an ice cream; you scream and get one. You want to break things; you scream, and you're allowed to break things. And so on. But life with no constraints tends to end pretty early.

Some time ago we worked with an executive who was highly dominant and overbearing. We observed her in meetings both with groups of people and with individuals. If she could get away with dominating people, she did, and being very senior, the situation appeared to her to allow the behaviour. But the performance in her area of the business was declining and people in the division she ran were quitting for other jobs. The pressure was building on her to turn things around.

When faced with new situations people tend to do what worked for them in the past, despite the fact that the behaviour may no longer be appropriate. They continue to indulge their preferential behaviour and ignore the demands of the situation. This executive was no exception, but when we talked things through with her and provided her with hard data feedback, it became clear to her that if she was going to improve the performance in her business unit she needed to change her behaviour quite substantially.

Needless to say, she didn't like what the data told her because it was not how she preferred to behave. But faced with the facts, she recognized that if she was going to succeed she had to act differently. There's little doubt she didn't find it easy – or enjoyable – but she did change her behaviour quite radically, and she turned things around successfully. *Her personality never changed, but her behaviour did.* It was her *behaviour,* not her personality, that drove her performance and results.

However, before we're tempted to throw the baby out with the bathwater, there are some personality traits that research shows have an effect on performance.

One of the more interesting ones is optimism, which can be thought of as confidence about the successful outcome of something, or as psychologists define it, the extent to which people have favourable expectations about their future. Research shows that optimism is related to health and longevity. [98] A study at the University of Pennsylvania looked at 25-year-old graduates and rated them with regard to optimism or pessimism. Follow-up with these individuals between the ages of 45 and 60 showed that those who were more pessimistic at 25 were more likely to be ill. Another study found that optimists who had coronary bypass surgery recovered faster than pessimists.[99] Optimists deal with stress better than pessimists, they are less subject to depression, and they are generally healthier.[100]

Christine Porath and associates talk about the concept of thriving, which they define as "the psychological state in which individuals experience both a sense of vitality and learning".[101] They describe vitality as "the sense of being alive, passionate, and excited", and learning as "the growth that comes from gaining new knowledge and skills".[102] They found that individuals who demonstrated the characteristics of thriving showed 16% better performance, 46% more satisfaction with their jobs, and 32% more commitment to the organization.[103] Friedrich Nietzsche put it this way, "He who has a *why* to live for can bear with almost any *how*".

Research also shows that two dimensions of personality – emotional stability and ambition (an aspect of extraversion) – have an effect on the ability to adapt behaviour to changing circumstances.[104] The second dimension, ambition, has an effect on **pro**active adaptation – i.e. freely taking the initiative to change. (We call this changing due to seeing the light.) An example is the performance of extravert CEOs making acquisitions. Acquisitions are commonly seen as one-sided affairs, but each one requires a different approach and strategy. The ability to adapt to these differences is a key to success, and research shows that extraverted CEOs make more successful acquisitions.[105] The first dimension, emotional stability, has an effect on **re**active adaptation – i.e. changing where the circumstances are forcing it. (We call this changing due to feeling the heat.)

Personality is stable

Personality is what you are. It is generally accepted that personality is established early in life and that it doesn't change much over time. A major study published in 2003 showed that the personalities of a thousand children in New Zealand (a sample size that makes the conclusions of the study pretty well bullet-proof) tested at age three, and then re-tested more than twenty years later, *had not changed.*[106] It appears that behavioural preferences are set as early as the age of three and they don't change much after that.

How personality develops is the subject of a seemingly never-ending debate about nature vs. nurture. Is personality a matter of genetics or is it something that develops through experiences and learning? There are research studies on both sides of the issue, although the majority fall on the side of nurture. [107] [108]

An issue that touches on the nature-nurture argument is birth order. Does birth order determine personality? The popular belief is that it does, but research with 20,000 people showed no difference in extroversion, emotional stability, agreeableness, conscientiousness, self-reported intellect, IQ, imagination, or openness to experience that was in any way related to birth order.[109]

Given that personality remains constant, why do organizations continue to use personality testing to determine whether to hire people? Presumably they imagine (incorrectly as we have shown) some sort of match between a consistent type of behaviour and a certain personality profile, and because they are looking for that type of behaviour for the job in question they choose an individual who has what they see as the appropriate personality.

However, even if we were to assume that there is a consistent link between an individual's personality and behaviour (which there isn't), an immutable fact of all organizational life is that *jobs change continually.* What happens when the behaviour necessary to managing the changed job is no longer the type of behaviour that the personality profile matches? Is the individual now obsolete? Does the organization have to begin another search for the "right" personality for the new job?

Clearly the process is nonsense. If successful performance is the result of doing the right things at the right time, and the "right" things change as the job changes but personality remains fixed, it is impossible to conclude that personality determines performance.

*Personality is what you **are**,* and it appears you can't change it to any significant degree. *Behaviour is what you **do**,* and you can most definitely change that.

Why do people change their behaviour?

But why do you change your behaviour? Is it purely a matter of whim? Is it random? Clearly not. It's because of the situation which confronts you. You behave differently when you're with a group of people whom you like than you do when you're with a group of people whom you dislike. Soldiers act differently when they're on duty and when they're off duty. People behave differently at a party than when they're at home. You behave differently at work than you do on holiday.

In a work context, the situation changes relatively constantly and if you want to perform effectively, you have to change your behaviour to match it. *The situation drives behaviour and behaviour drives performance.* For instance, if your preference is for orderliness, tidiness and predictability and you live alone with no external pressures to act differently, you will make sure your living space is neat, tidy and orderly. This is your personal preference driving your behaviour with no constraints on that behaviour. If you then enter into a serious relationship and your partner is casual and untidy, and if you want the relationship to continue, the situation forces you to relax your focus on tidiness and orderliness to some degree and to act a bit more casually – i.e. in a non-preferred manner. The situation is driving your behaviour and performance.

To give another example, if you're an extravert and you prefer to be outgoing and dominant you don't *have* to act that way all the time. Think about times when you've been invited to a meeting where the people involved are senior to you, or more experienced than you, or have much more technical knowledge than you, and where the agenda concerns something that involves experience and knowledge that you don't hold in abundance. If you're an extravert who likes to speak out, do you attempt to do that in this particular meeting? Not if you have any sense at all. You adapt your behaviour to the situation.

Apart from the fact, as we pointed out earlier, that you can't trust the results of personality tests because 75% of people get different results when they complete a test a second time, personality typing also has another downside. It often gives people an excuse *not* to adapt their behaviour to changing situations. "I'm not good at detail. It says so in my personality profile. So you just have to understand that I can't deal with a job that requires attention to detail." Nonsense. If that individual were trapped in a burning building and it was necessary to perform some detailed operation to get out they'd be able to focus on the minutest of detail.

Behaviour and personality (if measured accurately) are complementary

Understanding your personality is useful because it gives you an indication of the *range* of behaviour within which you are more likely to operate comfortably and effectively. While no one can expect to be able to go through life and work being able to behave solely within a tightly defined range, completely indulging a few behavioural preferences, it is helpful for you to understand what jobs or roles sit so far outside your behavioural preference comfort zone that engaging in them will lead to conflict, unhappiness and an increased probability of failure.

To give an example, we worked with a large multinational company on a project designed to help people find jobs and roles in which they would be most effective. First, a team of industrial psychologists used a set of personality diagnostics that showed individuals the range of behaviours with which they would likely be comfortable. Then, using our behavioural diagnostics we showed them the behaviours they were using to manage their current jobs. And finally, once again using our diagnostics, we showed them the behaviours on which they would need to focus to perform their prospective jobs effectively.

This allowed them to see whether jobs they thought they would like were within their preferential behaviour range – i.e. whether they had at least some preference for the behaviour required by the new job.

If someone enjoys doing something they tend to do more of it, and they tend to get better at it. In other words, their performance improves. If they have to consistently do things they don't enjoy, they tend to do less of them, and their performance decreases (Thorndike's *Law of Effect*). Ed Schein talks about this in what he calls *Career Anchors*.[110] He defines a career anchor as "a combination of perceived areas of competence, motives and values that you would not give up". Career anchors are tied (no pun intended) to the self-concept – a person's sense of who and what they are, a sense of "me". As such they are a manifestation of personality. In terms of work they are the things that define you to yourself, that are your strongest preferences, and which you are least willing to forego.

We researched the effectiveness of several hundred managers in a large multinational over a three-year period. All of them went through a half day of psychometric testing and all the information about their jobs – functions, level, job history, etc. – was provided.

We tracked who got promoted, who didn't, and who left (resigned or got fired) and were able to quantify the data and create an algorithm that predicted with 85%+ accuracy who would be promoted and who would not. The interesting thing was that *personality characteristics accounted for almost none of the variance.* The main predictors were situational factors and the individuals' ability to adjust their behaviour appropriately.[111] We live in an age of continuous and rapid situational change. The requirements of your job are never going to remain static. So if you continue to behave purely in terms of your personality preferences you're in trouble.

Unfortunately, as the neuroscientist Dean Burnett remarks, "the most worrying and wide-spread use of personality tests is in the corporate world" and regrettably they are applied by what he describes as "non-scientific types who don't know better and have been caught up in the hype".[112]

If you intend to use personality inventories, or have been asked or made to undergo one, make sure you do a little research and that you look for the inventory's level of validity. "Validity" is about the degree to which the instrument measures what it says it measures. In other words, can you rely on the results? A test is valid if it predicts outcomes that matter. Tests in popular magazines or tabloid papers that purport to do things like measure your sex appeal have no validity. The test may show you to be as hot as a pistol, but the real test is whether other people think that. Many of the most widely used personality inventories have little or no validity.

The second thing to look at is reliability. Reliability – often referred to as test-retest reliability – is the measure of whether you get the same results when you do the test again. If you keep getting different results, it's telling you something.

Adam Grant, an organizational psychologist and professor at the University of Pennsylvania, takes particular aim at the most widely used personality test, the Myers-Briggs Type Indicator (MBTI), and says that it is "about as useful as a polygraph for detecting lies".[113] The eminent neuroscientist Dean Burnett, whom we quoted earlier, says "The MBTI is not supported or approved by the scientific community ... it's based on untested decades-old assumptions put together by enthusiastic amateurs, working from a single source ... it now has hundreds of thousands of proponents who swear by it. But then, so do horoscopes".[114]

If you want to use a personality test with good validity, look at what we believe to be the best available – meaning the most valid and the most reliable: *The Saville Wave.*

Key points from this chapter

- Personality predicts, at most, only 15% of behaviour

- Nobody behaves the same way in all contexts; the situation matters

- The principal factor determining people's behaviour is the situation in which they find themselves, and their behaviour changes as the situation changes

- Be careful about what personality tests tell you. Research shows that 75% of people get a different result when they do a personality test again

- Personality is how you *prefer* to behave, given no constraints

- One personality characteristic, optimism – the extent to which people have favourable expectations about their future – is related to good health and longevity

- It is generally accepted that personality is established early in life and that it doesn't change much over time

- The situation drives behaviour and behaviour drives performance

- Having some understanding of your basic personality preferences gives you an indication of the range of behaviour within which you can operate comfortably and effectively, and can help you avoid jobs where you are not likely to be happy

- If you're going to use a personality test, do a little research and check its validity – the degree to which it measures what it says it measures, its accuracy

4

SECRET 3

Highly Effective Leadership
is about the situation

"Just because you're the right manager for certain circumstances it does not mean you're the right manager for another set of circumstances"

KEITH HAMILL

The biggest influence on behaviour and performance is the situation. The organizational world is littered with people who failed because they didn't adjust their behaviour to the changed or changing situation. And in most cases, it wasn't because that they didn't want to change, it was because they didn't recognize why they had to. But, as Rich Frank, former chairman of Walt Disney Television and Telecommunications, so colourfully phrases it, "if you're not part of the steamroller, you're part of the road".

The Wall Street Journal announced the departure of the CEO of Barnes and Noble in 2016 with a story in which it reported the board of the company as saying he "was not a good fit for the organization and that it was in the best interests of all parties for him to leave the company".[115] In plain language, the situation facing Barnes and Noble had changed and the board didn't think the CEO had adapted to it adequately.

Research done by Booz Allen about executive turnover in the world's largest 2,500 companies showed that CEOs who came from outside the organization were fired twice as frequently as those that came from inside (35% vs. 18.5%).[116] McKinsey says that the general rate of executive failure, not just CEOs, when moving to a new role has remained constant over the past 15 years at around 40%.[117] The principal reason is that they've come into a new and different situation and haven't been able to adapt to it quickly enough.

As we pointed out earlier, when faced with new situations, people tend to do what worked for them in the past, despite the fact that the behaviour may no longer be appropriate. They don't recognize the different demands of the new situation. The problem is that what worked in situation A is not necessarily what works in situation B.

We followed the careers and behaviour of around a hundred managers in a Canadian electric utility company for a period of seven years and asked them to complete a behaviour questionnaire at the end of every year and/or each time they changed jobs. Those managers who changed their behaviour to meet the changing demands of the industry and their jobs maintained an upwardly mobile career pattern. Those who failed to change their behaviour over a period of time either remained stagnant in their jobs or lost them. Peter Drucker said that "The most common cause of executive failure is the inability or unwillingness to change with the demands of a new position".[118]

A colleague of ours, Alejandro Serralde studied the effects of leader behaviour on employee ratings of working conditions, working relationships, immediate managers and senior management.[119] The study involved 103 managers and 1,348 non-supervisory staff. Findings showed that the greater the ability of managers to change their behaviour to align with situational changes affecting the organization, the higher the level of overall job satisfaction of staff.

Bloomberg Business Week reports that the average life expectancy of all firms, regardless of size, is 12.5 years. They make the point that companies that endure are sensitive to changes in the business environment and are able to adapt to these changes. Change in the 21st century is blindingly fast, and failure to adapt means declining performance, and sometimes outright catastrophe. For instance, when the category killer, the smartphone, was introduced, it took Nokia's market share in mobile phones from 46% in 2007 to 3% in 2013.

But regardless of whether the situational change is fast or slow, no jobs stay the same for any length of time. At a *conscious* level, we may not notice the changes, but at a *subconscious* level we do. The pre-frontal cortex (PFC) is the most evolved section of the brain, and it enables us to alter our actions and strategies as the situation we face changes – if we let it. However, while subconsciously we see everything, as Daniel Kahneman points out in his excellent book *Thinking, Fast and Slow*, our conscious brain prefers to take a lazier approach, and overlooks things that may require more effort or thought. [120]

Being alert to tiny incremental changes takes effort, so we concentrate on what is more obvious and immediate, and we miss the miniscule changes that are constantly occurring. Change is often gradual and imperceptible. It's like trees growing: you don't notice the day-to-day change. It's only after the duration of years that it becomes apparent that the roots of the lovely group of willows you planted for shade in your backyard have begun to crack and crumble the foundations of your house.

Think about the job you're doing now and what your job was twelve months ago. Think about what's remained the same and what's changed. The list of things that have changed – the different things you now have to do to perform your job well – will surprise you. If you think that you're on top of your job right now and you couldn't do it any better, you've probably just fallen behind.

Everyone knows the parable of the frog. If one is sadistic enough (and presumably some experimenter was) to put a frog in a pot of warm water and then slowly heat the water, the frog will not detect the incremental temperature change and will boil to death. The implication is that we're just like frogs. But we don't have to be. While the frog may not have processes at its command that allow it to monitor the very slow temperature change, we do. The slow and lazy part of the brain, the conscious part, may not recognize changes, but the very, very fast subconscious brain can, and does.

Understanding the changing situation – and dealing with it effectively

Jobs are different from one another, not simply in terms of having different descriptions or mandates, but in terms of demanding different types of behaviour from the individual doing them in order to perform effectively.

For instance, some jobs require long-term planning, while others need rapid reaction to changing circumstances. Some jobs require the leader to give clear and detailed instructions to people who lack experience while other jobs only require the person to provide goals and targets to skilled and experienced individuals. Some jobs require strict compliance with process and procedure. Others require constant monitoring of changing circumstances and competitive actions, and require rapid adjustment to deal with them.

Jobs change continually. A new responsibility is added, a new problem surfaces, a new person joins the team, a new system is introduced, new pressures arise, a competitor does something different, objectives change, and so on. The changes are often incremental, and we tend not to notice them. But they are cumulative, and they can have a strong bearing on the behaviours and actions most appropriate for dealing with them.

As the key behaviours required for high performance in your job change you can only continue to perform effectively if you do some things differently, or if you do some different things.

Traditionally we've thought about jobs in terms of their goals and objectives (KPIs – Key *Performance* Indicators), but research shows that achieving the KPIs requires focusing on a small number of Key *Behaviour* Indicators (K**B**Is) - the specific actions needed to deliver results. KPIs are about the "what" of a job. K**B**Is are about the "how'".

As the diagram below illustrates, the greater the match between your actions and what the situation demands (the KBIs), the greater your effectiveness.

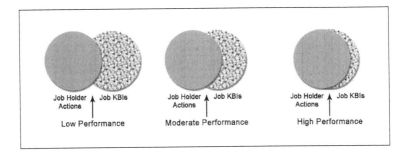

A lot of what makes up "the situation" is people, their perceptions, emotions, values, beliefs, needs, relationships, etc. Situational sensitivity involves emotional intelligence. Emotional intelligence is about understanding your emotions (self-awareness), and about managing your emotions. It's also about emotional self-control (delaying gratification and suppressing impulsiveness), and empathy (recognizing emotions in others).[121]

Emotional intelligence is a highly important component of leader effectiveness.[122] It is much more important than IQ or personality.[123] The Anglo-Saxon root of the words lead, leadership and leader is "*laed*", which means path or road. A leader's behaviour is aimed at getting people to follow that road. Sometimes the road is straight and easy and there's a promise of an ice cream stand at the end (or if you're past the age of being interested in ice cream and would prefer a good drink, perhaps a nice bar). But the leader needs to understand that not everyone is enticed by the prospect of ice cream or cocktails. The better you understand people and are able to empathise with them, the more likely you are to be effective as a leader.

Of course, situational changes also involve things like technology, demographics, the economy, politics, and so on. For example, the recreational vehicle (RV) industry is highly sensitive to situational changes, so much so that RV sales are considered a leading economic indicator. Situational factors affecting RV sales are things like the price of fuel and employment, and traditionally, as these two things have risen or fallen, sales have moved in the same direction.

A good example of spotting a major situational change and taking the right actions at the right time is Randy Potts, who in 2011 became CEO of Winnebago, a company *Fortune* calls "the brontosaurus of consumer vehicles". The change Potts noted was what's referred to in the US as the Silver Tsunami – 76 million baby-boomers in the prime age group of RV buyers, the largest group of retirees in US history. Given this situation Potts introduced a new line of vehicles that are specifically targeted to meet the Silver Tsunami's desire for nostalgia combined with modern comfort. Sales have gone from $211 million in 2009 to pushing $900 million in 2015.

Situational Distortion and Power

Is there such a thing as a "benevolent autocrat"? Some economists think so, but their view of "benevolence" is often rather stretched. The 19th century British aristocrat, Baron Acton, is famously quoted as saying "Power tends to corrupt, and absolute power corrupts absolutely". To give Acton his due he did say "tends to" because even though it does more often than not, it doesn't always do so.

In the Western world, people tend to see power as something bad (unless, of course, they have it). As a result, it doesn't generally get good press. But if you think of power as the level of control over your things in your life, it's a highly positive thing. For starters, it's linked to longevity and health – the greater control you have over your work, the longer you're likely to live.[124]

At the other end of the spectrum, low, or no control over the work environment is a huge producer of stress, and prolonged high levels of stress can cause hypertension and heart disease, impaired immunity, diabetes, depression, and even things as seemingly mundane as colds.[125]

Positional power

Positional power is the power that an individual gets because of a role or position. The power may be specified by the position or it may be assumed. In general, a president has more power than a vice-president, a manager more power than a supervisor, an admiral more power than a captain, a cardinal more power than a bishop, etc. But there are job titles that are somewhat amorphous; for instance, where does a "Change Leader" or Equality Champion" stand in the power hierarchy?

Positional power is a situational element that affects behaviour. We know that people act differently towards those whom they perceive to have higher power and status than themselves. You act differently with your boss than you do with a work colleague or a social friend. And of course, we also recognize that people often act differently towards others of lower power. So it's safe to say that power, whether assumed or actual, can change behaviour.

But how about this? Did you know that the reverse also holds true: behaviour can change power? To explain the dynamics of how that works let's start with an experiment with an aggressive species of fish, green sunfish. [126]

Researchers divided a group of the fish into three subgroups for five days. One group went into isolation, a second was put into a tank with bigger fish (by definition, stronger and more dominant), and the third group into a tank with some smaller fish. After five days the green sunfish were brought back together in one tank. The group that had been with the smaller fish became more aggressive and dominant. The group that had been with the big fish became less aggressive. Behaviour changed power. Winning behaviour – beating up smaller fish – increased power, and losing behaviour – being beaten up by a bigger fish – decreased it.

So, if it works with fish, what about humans? Ian Robertson, professor of psychology at Trinity College Dublin, gives a human example of this phenomenon with the come-back career of heavyweight boxer Mike Tyson.[127] After Tyson's three years in jail, his manager, Don King, knew all about how behaviour affects power and made sure that Tyson's first come-back fights would successively result in decisive wins. (In boxing parlance this is called the "Tomato Can Effect". A "tomato can" is defined as "a lousy fighter who usually loses to experienced boxers in 4 or 5 rounds"). By the time Tyson got to fight Frank Bruno for the heavyweight title, he'd had a series of wins. Like the sunfish that had experienced success dominating smaller fry, the victories changed his behaviour and made him more aggressive and confident. He knocked Bruno down in the first round, knocked him onto the ropes several times subsequently, and the fight ended in the fifth round when it was stopped by the referee, with Tyson declared the winner.

What is happening here to explain this behaviour change? For starters, winning increases testosterone in the blood stream and that alters the chemistry of the brain.[128] The way it does this is to increase dopamine, a neurotransmitter, and dopamine drives action-centredness. It affects the motivation to get something you want, and it drives behaviour to achieve that. It also increases the appetite for risk.

But you don't have to personally win to get the testosterone increase or decline. Some fascinating research was done in 1994 by a group of researchers from Georgia State University about the effects of *vicarious* winning and losing.[129] The final of the Football (soccer) World Cup in 1994 was between Italy and Brazil. Each team had won the cup three times; this was a clash of the titans. Italy had lost in the semi-final four years before but were the favourites in 1994. Before the game, the researchers from Georgia State took saliva samples from a group of Brazilian fans in a sports bar and a group of Italian fans in another location. Immediately after the game they took samples from the groups again.

The game ended in a shoot-out. Brazil took the first shot and failed. Italy took the next shot and also failed. The next two Brazilians scored, as did the next two Italians. Then the fourth Brazilian scored, making them 3-2 up. The fourth Italian shooter missed but they were allowed five shots. The fifth shooter would tie the match. It was Roberto Baggio. Italy would never have reached the final without Baggio. He was a superstar. He had scored five goals during the tournament. But Baggio missed the final attempt at goal and Italy lost the World Cup 3-2.

The results of the researchers' testing were absolutely dramatic. After the end of the game the average level of testosterone of the Brazilian fans had risen by 28%. So vicarious victory has a direct effect on the brain's chemistry. But so does vicarious loss. The average testosterone levels of the Italian fans *dropped* by 27%.

Some downsides of power

There are also downsides to power and the changes to the brain it brings about. Because power increases the level of testosterone, it tends to block out various things seen as peripheral. It acts to some degree like a set of blinkers. It also de-sensitises you to others. When your levels of testosterone rise you become more ego-centric and are less inclined to listen to or accept others' points of view. Research done by Adam Galinsky and colleagues showed that high-power people are less adept at reading other's emotions, less inclined to accept the ideas and views of others, and less adept at understanding others' feelings, thinking or perceptions. [130]

And further studies showed that as people's power feelings were aroused they tended to increasingly see other people as objects in terms of their usefulness rather than their human qualities.[131] Using wealth as a proxy for power, a study of the behaviour of shoppers at high-end, expensive outlets, showed that when they were faced with a stranger requiring help they were less inclined to help (35%) than shoppers at ordinary lower-price places (77.5%).[132]

Research also indicates that powerful people perform badly in teams.[133] Teams made up of entirely high-power individuals, entirely low-power individuals, and teams with a mix of the two, were given a task involving creativity. The teams were videotaped as they engaged the task and the tapes were rated by independent judges on creativity, conflict, task focus, information sharing, and positive interactions. The teams composed purely of high-powered individuals had fewer positive interactions and shared less information than the low-power or mixed teams.

Fortunately, we aren't completely ruled by a testosterone-dopamine-fuelled rush for winning at all cost. In the right half of the brain's pre-frontal cortex the hormone that makes the difference is noradrenaline (known in the USA as norepinephrine). It stimulates the brain to be alert to threat and the response to threat.[134] Instead of being focused and blinkered, its view is wide and inclusive. Antelope on the Serengeti plain are alert to the dangers posed by the big beasts and the signals they give out. In organizations it also pays to be alert to the "big beasts" who have the power to curtail or end careers.

If you're in a position of power – a "Big Beast" of some kind – be very aware of the signals you send. Like the antelope on the plains, people are highly sensitive to all your actions and comments. Take the advice of Niall Fitzgerald, former chairman of Unilever, who says, "One of the things that leaders don't fully recognize is that when they speak or act they are speaking into an extraordinary amplification system". A casual remark can have unintended dramatic consequences. One thinks of Henry II's remark to a group of his courtiers, "Will no one rid me of this troublesome priest?" which they took as a request to kill Thomas Becket, the Archbishop of Canterbury.

A personal memory we have is of the chief executive of a company with which we were involved saying something like "I don't know why we keep people like X", the result being that a sycophantic executive in whose division X worked, took it on himself to have the individual fired.

Does power alone make an individual aggressive and domineering? Does a series of wins over weaker opponents explain it? Organizations are hierarchical and if you're the boss, generally speaking your views get accepted more than those of people below you. Will you automatically become aggressive when you get into a position of power?

Fortunately, not. At least not if you are comfortable with your level of skills and knowledge (although everyone, you included, experiences doubts from time to time about that sort of thing). Research shows that aggression is linked to feelings of incompetence.[135] And interestingly, it appears that individuals who engage in abusive behaviour feel less fulfilled by their workday and feel less autonomous, less competent, and less able to relate to others.[136] They have a "power hangover".

Key points from this chapter

- The biggest influence on behaviour and performance is the situation

- Whether the situational change is fast or slow, no jobs stay the same for any length of time

- As the key behaviours required for high performance in your job change you can only continue to perform effectively if you do some things differently, or if you do some different things

- The greater the match between your actions and what the situation demands (the KBIs), the greater your effectiveness

- The greater control you have over your work, the longer you're likely to live

- Low or no control over the work environment is a huge producer of stress, resulting in a weakened immune system, diabetes, depression, and even things as seemingly mundane as colds

- Understanding situations involving people – and most organizational situations involve people – requires a level of emotional intelligence: understanding your emotions, managing your emotions, emotional self-control, and empathy

- Positional power is a situational element that affects behaviour – people act differently towards those whom they perceive to have either higher or lower power and status than themselves

- Behaviour can change power. Winning increases testosterone in the blood stream and that alters the chemistry of the brain by increasing dopamine, and dopamine drives action-centredness

- Because power increases the level of testosterone, it acts to some degree like a set of blinkers, blocking out various thing, and it de-sensitises you to others

- As people's power feelings are aroused they tend to increasingly see other people as objects in terms of their usefulness rather than their human qualities

- Powerful people tend to perform badly in teams

5

SECRET 4

Highly Effective Leadership is about motivation

If you don't enjoy what you are doing, you are going to have a hard time doing it well and being successful

DAVID QUILTY

Motivation is one of those words, a bit like personality, that is popularly used in a variety of ways. The psychology definition is "the process that initiates, guides, and maintains goal-oriented behaviours". Which is a bit like defining hunger as something that occurs when you're hungry. It's a drive that makes you want to do something, and if that something turns out to be rewarding in some fashion, it makes you want to repeat the action.

Do leaders motivate people? The overwhelming majority of books, articles, or so-called experts say yes. But this view, as Jeffrey Pfeffer says, "is almost mechanical – (it's that) if you want employees to do something, they need either positive inducements, or threats or punishments. In the absence of some external force, it seems to be assumed that people would be inert, just like objects in Newtonian physics where a body at rest will remain at rest unless impelled by some force into motion."[137]

What Pfeffer describes isn't motivation, it's what Fred Herzberg called "movement".[138] He said that when a manager tries to "motivate" someone, it's actually the *manager* who is motivated (i.e. wants someone to do something) and it is the individual who "moves" (does the something). He describes the process as being similar to training a dog to do things by giving it treats. When it rolls over, sits down, or whatever the trainer wants it to do, it gets a treat. The trainer is the one who's motivated – who wants the actions performed. The dog just "moves" – does the tricks – and most importantly, only does them when the reward is on offer. When there is no reward on offer, no dog tricks occur.

So the real answer to whether leaders motivate people is "No". Motivation isn't something you *do* to someone. People motivate themselves; they do things for various reasons, often known only to them. However, leaders can create and facilitate the conditions that *enable* people to become motivated. They can do that by structuring jobs, tasks, projects, and goals in such a way that people engage them with enthusiasm. When people do things with enthusiasm they're motivated, but when they do them passively and routinely, they're just moving.

Vince Lombardi, the legendary American football coach's expression was: "If you're not fired with enthusiasm you'll be fired with enthusiasm". However, it appears that the majority of employees are not enthusiastic about their jobs. Gallup's annual survey of how satisfied and engaged people are with their jobs found that in 2016 only 33% defined themselves as "engaged". More than half were "not engaged". Gallup describes being "not engaged" this way: "These employees are not hostile or disruptive. They show up and kill time, doing the minimum required with little extra effort to go out of their way for customers. They are less vigilant, more likely to miss work and change jobs when new opportunities arise. They are thinking about lunch or their next break. Not engaged employees are either 'checked out' or attempting to get their job done with little or no management support".[139]

Even more distressing is the fact that of 80,884 individuals surveyed by Gallup, 17% were "*actively* disengaged". These people are defined as hostile, and not just unproductive but actively attempting to undermine the work of others, spreading feelings of negativity, and sabotaging output and productivity.

Is money a motivator?

There are any number of theories of motivation, either put forward by academics or drawn from what can best be described as the "what I know to be the fact because I've seen it work with people" school of so-called common-sense knowledge. In the organizational world, the carrot and stick theory is one of those, money being the usual carrot, and being disciplined or fired from the job, the stick.

People certainly do things for money. For instance, the website www.money.howstuffworks.com lists the top dirty job (and it's a *very* dirty job) as crime scene cleaner. But people do it because it pays well - $75,000+ a year. Much of what we see and read reinforces the conclusion that money is what motivates people to work. Professional players in virtually every team sport – football, American football, baseball, rugby, basketball, and so on – happily move from one team to another for greater earnings. But is the move about money or prestige? The more you're being paid, the more you're worth, and everyone likes to think they are valuable and have prestige.

Money as a motivator is a highly complex concept because it stands as a proxy for many different things. It's used as a measure of success, achievement, social standing, and for the ability to demonstrate all these things. *The Financial Times* produces a supplement called "How to Spend it" which is about using money to buy things that give you showing-off and bragging rights.

A McKinsey survey asked respondents to rate three non-financial motivators – praise from immediate manager, attention from a leader, and a chance to lead a project or task force – against three highly rated financial incentives – cash bonuses, increased base pay, and stock or stock options. The non-financial incentives were all rated as more effective motivators than the financial incentives.[140]

A mountain of research evidence points to the fact that external incentives like salary, bonuses, benefits, or even "negative incentives" like threats, have little or no lasting impact on effort or performance. An old video of Fred Herzberg's illustrates this wonderfully. A manager is talking to an employee, trying to get her enthused about her work. He reminds her of the bonus she got, the special desk chair her got for her, the extra time off he gave her, etc. Her reply is "So what have you done for me lately?"

Follow the money

A lot of people would point to industries like banking as an example of money motivating behaviour. People in investment banks appear to be there purely for the high levels of monetary reward. For instance, the average tenure of a managing director (MD) at Goldman Sachs is 8.5 years.[141] If the average age of someone becoming an MD is 35 that means they are out of the job before they're 45, and we presume the motivation is to then have enough money not to have to work.

The norm in large banks like Goldman Sachs, Morgan Stanley and Bank of America Merrill Lynch was a 70-80-hour work week, with "all-nighters" being the mark of outstanding commitment. However, working long hours purely for the sake of it, or to give the impression of being highly productive, has in fact precisely the opposite effect. James Surowiecki points out that, "long hours diminish both productivity and quality ... for knowledge workers fatigue and sleep-deprivation make it hard to perform at a high cognitive level".[142]

Research shows that overwork "decreases cognitive flexibility in problem solving and performance on a complex task with difficult goals", and, more disturbing, that monetary rewards decrease intrinsic motivation.[143] Also, the hype promoting the benefits of multi-tasking is dangerously wrong. In fact, the competition for attention, and what psychologists call fractured stimulus, tires the brain and causes a breakdown of the self-control mechanisms that prevent you from taking risky or ill-advised actions that you would not normally take.[144]

Once again, we're led to the conclusion that it must be the money that gets people to behave this way. But the finance business is unique in that it's purely about money. It doesn't manufacture anything, it doesn't make people healthier, it doesn't move goods and services around, it makes (or loses) money. So if that's what it's about, then that's what people in the business are attracted to and motivated by.

However, you need to be careful about what behaviour monetary incentives can cause. Often the results are not what was intended. A recent example is what happened when Wells Fargo set up an incentive system for its employees to open new accounts. The idea behind the program makes sense because it's about growing the customer base. However, it led to employees opening 1.5 million bank accounts and applications for 565,000 credit cards that were not authorised by customers. One customer in Southern California had seven unauthorised accounts opened in his name and three debit cards issued.[145]

The three most fundamental and powerful motivators

This book is about what hard-nosed, scientifically structured research shows are the actualities. And when it comes to what motivates people and what leaders need to do to create change and sustain the momentum for achieving it, there are three critical fundamentals.[146]

Recognition

Recognition has a strong positive effect on performance.[147] The more people are given recognition and appreciation, the higher their levels of motivation and performance.[148] It makes you feel good about yourself and to believe that your performance has value.[149] Research shows that just simply saying "Thank you" to someone has a powerful effect on their self-esteem and performance.[150] Napoleon said, "A soldier will fight long and hard for a bit of colored ribbon". Recognition, and the associated feeling of reward triggers the release of the hormone dopamine from several sites in the brain.[151] Surges of dopamine in the brain create a feeling of pleasure and reward.

One of the interesting things is that the effects of the dopamine are significantly stronger when the recognition is unexpected. When you expect to be recognized for something, and are, it's highly motivating, but when you don't expect it, it's even more so.[152]

In the current tight job market in the US a new problem has emerged in the fast food industry – retaining employees – and some enlightened individuals have realised the importance of recognition. Eddie Rodriguez, who operates 177 Wendy's in Florida, New Mexico and Texas, is one. He says, "Today's employee, they want to feel wanted", and to demonstrate that he's gone at least part of the way and raised his stores' average hourly rate as a sign of recognition of their value. Terry Smith, owner of three McDonald's, says of his employees "if you treat them right and have a vested interest in them, they'll stick around". [153] At last, it seems, the realisation has dawned on managers that people want to feel they have some worth and are valued and respected.

Doug Chung and Das Narayandas, two Harvard Business School academics, studied the effects of a bonus system for sales people and the central finding was that results varied depending on whether individuals felt they had to do something to earn the bonus or they were just given it.[154] What that says is that money itself is not the motivator, it's representative of something else – in this case, recognition.

A somewhat off-beat study found that recognition and appreciation don't even have to be purposefully demonstrated either verbally or through specifically intended physical actions or gestures to have an effect on performance. Researchers set up four scenarios in a restaurant: (1) the baseline condition – diners and cooks out of sight of one another, (2) diners able to see cooks but not vice-versa, (3) cooks able to see diners but not vice-versa, and (4) both cooks and diners able to see one another.[155] When the cooks could see the customers, satisfaction with the food increased by 10%. When the diners and the cooks could both see one another satisfaction increased by 17.3% and service was 13% faster. The conclusion drawn by the researchers was that "Employees who observed customer transparency felt that their work was more appreciated and more impactful and thus were more satisfied with their work and more willing to exert effort".

Approval

The number one, most powerful, motivational driver is *approval* – how we are seen by others. Are we admired or envied, or even noticed? In a social sense approval can translate into status – how the society in which we live (the culture, the group, the community, the gang, etc.) rates and ranks us. Money can be a proxy for status and approval, but it's the approval that makes the difference.[156] A great line from the old movie *On the Waterfront* illustrates this wonderfully. The principal concern of the young boxer Terry Malloy, who has been made to throw a fight, is not about the money he could have had, it's about the approval and status: "I coulda had class. I coulda been a contender. I coulda been somebody".

What makes approval such a powerful motivator is the actual physical process that it triggers. It's not just something that makes you pleased by coincidence or accident, it's once again because of the action of the hormone dopamine. The interesting thing, however, is that while doing something well, or achieving something, increases the dopamine level, getting approval for it by a knowledgeable other (i.e. someone whose opinion is valued) *hugely* increases the surge of dopamine.

Recognition and approval are a very powerful central human need – they're about a sense of belonging, of being a part of something, of being included. Proof that this is such a strong element in our makeup is demonstrated by neurological research that shows that the areas of the brain that light up when the reverse occurs and a person feels ostracised are the same as those that are activated by physical pain.[157]

An interesting corollary to the idea that approval is a major motivator is that it also correlates to wellbeing and longevity. Approval bolsters the self-concept. While wealth plays a role in terms of health because it translates into things like healthier eating, higher levels of sanitation, better access to health care, etc., research indicates a positive correlation between social status (approval from others) and health and longevity.[158]

A quirky research finding about the link between approval and longevity is that Oscar winners live on average four years longer than Oscar nominees.[159] Just being nominated for an Oscar is a huge badge of approval, so it appears that there is no limit to the amount of approval we want. For actors, winning an Oscar is the pinnacle of status. It is the ultimate recognition and approval from knowledgeable others. But once again, showing that you simply can't get enough approval, multiple Oscar winners live an average of *six* years longer than nominees.

The effect even occurs in situations where the subject has been, for a significant period of time, the recipient of worldwide approval from the most discerning and distinguished "knowledgeable others". Nobel prize winners have all been recognized as being at the top of their fields for a long period of time, but once again, winners live, on average, two years longer than Nobel nominees.[160]

Another interesting fact is that the *anticipation* of recognition and approval is also a motivator. People spend more time, effort and resource if they have an opportunity to learn things. Knowledge has value and increases the sense of self-worth. Subjects in an experiment demonstrating this were given fMRI (functional magnetic resonance) scans while they read trivia questions. Their curiosity about the answers showed up as activity in a part of the brain known to relate to anticipated reward.[161] In other words, just the thought of being able to gain knowledge, even if only answers to trivia questions, (but who doesn't like to be able to quote some fact of which others aren't aware?) motivates behaviour.

There's a deep message here for leaders. *If you give people tasks where they have a chance to learn, they are more likely to be motivated and engaged than when they are given repetitive, rote tasks. And that can be taken further: money doesn't compensate for the lack of challenge and learning, it undermines motivation.* Research in 2010 showed that paying people for rote tasks actually undermined their motivation to perform the task. The researchers concluded that "the undermining effect is closely linked to a decreased sense of self-determination".[162]

A behavioural fact that runs as a consistent thread through everything this book is about is that people like to feel valued. They like to feel that their efforts and ideas are recognized as being of some significance and worth. That's something that a job can give to a person. Jobs provide a feeling of self-worth. The fact that you have a job means that someone believes you have something to contribute and have some value. Losing your job has an opposite effect. You might rationalise it as due to something out of your control, such as a company bankruptcy and dissolution, but you still need to find some other occupation that confers a sense of worth.

A research study conducted across 75 countries in the OECD, and published in *The Lancet,* describes the devastating effect of unemployment. "Unemployment rises were significantly associated with an increase in all-cancer mortality ... We estimate that the

2008-10 economic crisis was associated with about 260,000 excess cancer-related deaths in the OECD alone".[163]

Autonomy

The third most powerful motivator is autonomy – having control over what you do.[164] In its most potent form it's about doing things purely because you decide to, rather than doing things you feel in some way pressured to do. Individuals who are able to act on the basis of their own choice are more productive, are able to maintain persistent activity and focus, exhibit less stress and burnout, and generally experience higher levels of psychological well-being.[165] They have also been shown to have high energy at work, to feel mentally and physically strong, to perform better than other colleagues and show less stress.[166]

An experiment testing the effects of autonomy involved groups of children who were given a batch of attractive art supplies to play with. Some of the children were told that if they used the materials they would get a reward and others were left alone to play however they wished. When the same children, a week later, were again given similar materials to play with, the ones who had *not* been offered a reward engaged in playing with them much more eagerly than those who had been promised a reward. [167] We get more pleasure and enjoyment out of things when we take them on purely on our own initiative, rather than when they are presented by an external source with a condition.

Motivation comes from the job

Peter Drucker famously said "We know nothing about motivation. All we can do is write books about it". But for once Drucker was wrong. We *do* know something about motivation. *What we know is that, in an organizational context, motivation comes from the job.* [168]

Need for achievement

An individual's specific (motivational) needs are acquired over time and are shaped by their early life experiences. The great David McClelland identified three basic types of motivational need – the need for achievement, the need for affiliation, and the need for power. [169]

The need for achievement is basically the need to achieve goals and objectives that are challenging, and that earn approval – from others or from yourself, or both. People who have a high need for achievement display a number of differentiating characteristics. They like to be in situations where they are able to take personal responsibility for the outcome, and thereby to get personal satisfaction from their achievement. They tend to be less worried about what others think of them; they know what the goal was and they know whether they achieved it, and that's often quite enough. They don't like situations where the outcome is a matter of chance; it has to be affected by their own skill and effort. They set moderately high and challenging goals for themselves – not impossible goals and not goals that are easy to achieve. There has to be a sense of accomplishment – a provision of internal recognition and approval. Recognition, approval and autonomy are all in evidence.

And people with a high need for achievement also like and require consistent and concrete feedback on their performance. This is most important. They need to know how well or badly they're performing because without that data they can't either build on what's going well or correct what's going badly. Because of these characteristics, people with a high need for achievement are the most willing and able to change their behaviour. They will do what is needed to succeed.

Need for Affiliation

The need for affiliation is, in its most straightforward form, a desire to be liked by others, to be part of a group, to enter into warm, personal relationships with others, to be in the company of others. It's more about being popular or being liked than about performing at a high level or achieving the goals of the organization.

People with a high need for affiliation find it difficult to monitor and manage the behaviour and performance of others. They are reluctant to give negative feedback and they find it difficult to behave differently towards poorly performing individuals. They tend to shy away from making hard or controversial decisions or from expressing contentious views or opinions. They manage on the basis of personal relationships and their dopamine reward comes from the reciprocal warmth of these relationships. In terms of change, people with a high need for affiliation are the least willing to change their behaviour. When they do a cost-benefit analysis of changing behaviour vs. improving performance, the perceived cost of losing or destroying relationships often outweighs the perceived benefit of improved performance.

There is another behavioural consequence of a high need for affiliation that can occur. People with a high need for affiliation sometimes use the excuse of "people and their development are of prime importance to me and that's what makes me go out of my way to be helpful and supportive" as a screen to rationalise what can be rather toxic micro-management. Under the guise of "helping", they may actually maintain control by getting involved in the minutiae of whatever people are doing, by meddling, and by not giving others any authority or autonomy. Additionally, this behaviour has the unfortunate consequence of robbing people of recognition, approval and a sense of autonomy. David McClelland says, "Managers who are concerned about being liked tend to have subordinates who feel that they have little personal responsibility, believe that organizational procedures are not clear, and have little pride in their work group". [170]

Need for Power

In terms of leadership, perhaps the most important of McClelland's motivational drives for leaders to understand is the need for power (n-Power). The motivational need for power is not about autocratic, tyrannical behaviour; it's about the need to have some impact and influence on the achievement of organizational goals. It's about recognising that you get things done by influencing others.

People with a high need for achievement try to achieve results essentially on their own. But doing things on your own isn't leadership. It might set an example of what can be achieved, but by the central fact that it's purely personal and excludes the involvement of others, it's not motivating to them. It doesn't create a multiplicative effect.

High n-Power individuals, on the other hand, like to see results achieved through the efforts of others. They like the discipline of work, like to get things done in an orderly fashion, and they are more organization minded and feel responsible for building and strengthening their organizations. They put the interest of the organization ahead of their self-interest. They believe in hard work and sacrifice and think that people who show this behaviour should be rewarded for it. McClelland says "their positive self-image is not at stake in their jobs. They are less defensive, more willing to seek advice from experts, and have a longer-range view".[171]

McClelland differentiates between the need for personal power (p-power) and what he calls "socialized power" (s-power). S-power leaders are driven to achieve results for the wider benefit of others – their colleagues, their team, their organization. P-power leaders are driven to achieve results for personal benefit. Leaders who are high in p-power are, in many ways, the types of people who are characterised as being charismatic. George Patton, the World War II general is an example – huge ego, great energy, inspirational, personally driven and hard driving to his people. His rationale for his behaviour was "pressure makes diamonds". McClelland observes that because the subordinates of p-power leaders are loyal to them personally, rather than to the organization, when the leader leaves, things tend to fall apart.

S-power individuals make their people feel strong rather than weak, and engender a feeling of pride about working in the team. S-power individuals have their high need for power balanced by what McClelland calls inhibition – discipline and self-control. Lacking this sense of discipline and self-control, the p-power person tends to be aggressive and focused on self-aggrandisement, often characterised by the collection of symbols of prestige like fancy cars, extravagant offices, yachts, etc.

Perhaps McClelland's most interesting research finding, however, is that the key to predicting a leader's effectiveness is whether their power motivation is higher than their need for affiliation.[172] Using the output criteria of (1) sense of responsibility, (2) organizational clarity, and (3) team spirit as measures of leader effectiveness, he found that individuals with a high need for affiliation scored lowest on all three of these variables. Top performers were those who were high in s-Power. He found that they created high morale, produced a higher level of goal/value clarity, and generated a stronger bond with the organization.

If you put someone with a high need for achievement in a job where she is given sole responsibility for getting something done, where that is dependent on her skill and ability, and where she is provided with clear and continuous feedback on her performance, you'll get a highly motivated person who will do a great job.

If you put a person with a high need for affiliation in that type of job, they'll be turned off. The job you need to give them is one where they work with a group of people, where success is shared by the group, where they work together as friends and close colleagues, and where they all respect and like one another. Do not put them into a job where there is little or no contact with others.

If you put an individual with a high need for achievement in a job where he needs to influence a number of people in order to achieve something of a longer-term nature, and where feedback about progress towards the objective is difficult to pinpoint, he will tend to find it tough and stressful, and be unlikely to perform well.

If you're not enthusiastic about doing something, that means you don't enjoy it and you're not motivated by it, and you're not likely to do it well. If you don't do something well it's unlikely that you'll be rewarded. If you're not rewarded, you will tend to do less of it. The less you do of something the less proficient you tend to become at it. The less proficient you are at something the less chance you'll find it rewarding or be rewarded for doing it. And so on, in a continually downward spiral. The consequences aren't likely to be good.

However, if you enjoy doing something you create a positive upward spiral. If doing what you like (what motivates you) was a requirement of your job then presumably you would happily do a lot of it, do it well, and because you were doing it so well you would be more likely to be rewarded for your efforts. The recognition and approval for doing a good job would make you feel good about yourself and would increase your motivation. You would get a feeling of achievement from your efforts and you would experience a sense of growth as you became more and more expert and effective in your job. You might be given more responsibility and even get promoted. Having a motivating job leads to a lot of good things.

We call this the Seven Dwarfs Syndrome. As you recall, the Seven Dwarfs loved their work so much that they sang and whistled happily on their way *to* work. How many cheerful faces do you see on your way to work each day? People are generally silent and withdrawn, and smiles and laughter aren't common. Is the behaviour different at the end of the working day? Yes, the atmosphere is more relaxed, there is a hum of conversation and you hear laughter from time to time. Why can't this behaviour pattern be reversed? Why don't people whistle on the way to work and feel saddened when the day ends? Why isn't work satisfying and enjoyable. Why can't it give you a real feeling of accomplishment? Why can't we whistle on the way to work?

Key points from this chapter

- Motivation is a drive that makes you want to do something, and if that something turns out to be rewarding in some fashion, it makes you want to repeat the action

- Do leaders motivate people? No. Motivation isn't something you *do* to someone. People motivate themselves

- But leaders can create and facilitate the conditions that enable people to become motivated

- They can do that by things like structuring jobs, tasks, projects, and goals in such a way that people engage them with enthusiasm

  - Over 50% of employees are "not engaged", defined by behaviours like showing up and killing time, being less vigilant, being more likely to miss work and change jobs

  - Money as a motivator is a highly complex concept because it stands as a proxy for many different things

  - Research evidence points to the fact that external incentives like salary, bonuses, benefits, or even "negative incentives" like threats, have little or no lasting impact on effort or performance

  - Multi-tasking is not good and tires the brain and causes a breakdown of the self-control mechanisms that prevent you from taking risky or ill-advised actions that one would not normally take

  - The three most powerful motivators are
    - Approval
    - Recognition
    - Autonomy

  - Jobs provide a feeling of self-worth. The fact that you have a job means that someone believes you have something to contribute and have some value. Losing your job has an opposite effect. Loss of your job and unemployment are significantly associated with an increase in all-cancer deaths

  - The three basic motivational drives are:

- The need for achievement
    - The need for affiliation
    - The need for power

    - The need for achievement is the need to achieve goals and objectives that are challenging, and that earn approval – from others or from yourself, or both

    - The need for affiliation is a desire to be liked by others, to be part of a group, to enter into warm, personal relationships with others

    - The need for power is about the need to have some impact and influence on the achievement of organizational goals

    - There are two types of power motivation, the need for personal power (p-power) and (s-power). S-power leaders are driven to achieve results for the wider benefit of others – their colleagues, their team, their organization. P-power leaders are driven to achieve results for personal benefit

    - The key factor in predicting individuals' effectiveness is that their power motivation needs to be higher than their need for affiliation

    - Motivation comes from the job. If you enjoy what you're doing (are motivated by it) you will tend to do it well and be successful. If you don't enjoy what you are doing, the opposite is more likely. It's the Seven Dwarfs Syndrome.

6

SECRET 5

Highly Effective Leadership
is about values and culture

The only thing that works is management by values. Find people
who are competent and really bright, but more importantly,
people who care exactly about the same things you care about

STEVE JOBS

Research has consistently demonstrated that companies that focus on developing a strong set of corporate values over an extended period of time outperform companies that don't by a factor of *five to six times*.[173]

Organizations that are successful over the long term have clear values that are embedded and acted upon by people at all levels. Commonly accepted organizational values create a focused, consistent and unified approach to customers, to markets and to competition. They not only characterise the culture of the organization, they determine it.

Values are the beginning point and culture is the outcome – the enactment of the values. Culture is "the way we do things here", or as Geoff Colvin defines it, "the way people behave from moment to moment without being told". It is shaped by what gets rewarded and what gets punished or is ignored. And what gets rewarded, punished, or ignored is a reflection of the company's values – i.e. "what is valued around here and what isn't".

There are massive benefits that accrue from having core values to which everyone in the organization is committed. Research done by Peters and Waterman led them to conclude that one of the overarching benefits of commonly held values was that even at the lowest levels of an organization people "know what they are supposed to do in most situations because the handful of guiding values is crystal clear".[174] Research looking at how half a million workers in a variety of organizations viewed their employers showed that "firms with employees that maintain strong beliefs in the meaning of their work experience better (financial) performance".[175]

Most importantly from a leadership perspective, if everyone shares the same values you can feel confident that, faced with a decision, other people in the organization will act in a way that is consistent with what you would have done. You can feel comfortable about delegating responsibility more widely. You don't have to feel that you need to check on everything people are doing. If they hold the same values you hold, when they have to make a decision or take an action, they will ask themselves the same question you would ask: "If I do X, will that be consistent with our values?" You can sleep more soundly.

In case you think this is a pie-in-the-sky dream and that no organization works like that, take a look at Johnson & Johnson. They have what they call a Credo, a 300-word statement, written over 70 years ago by Robert Wood Johnson II, who took the company public. It sets out the core principles of the company and where its responsibilities lie. The Credo is a document that Johnson & Johnson uses throughout the organization to lay down ground rules for behaviour. It's displayed on the wall of every meeting room and in almost every office. During the year, in a variety of locations, executives from different operating companies get together in what is called the 'Credo Challenge'. During these one-or two-day meetings, business decisions are analysed in terms of how they uphold the principles in the Credo. The Credo is a living testament, not just words and it governs the way people in J&J behave. When current CEO Alex Gorsky presented his long-term vision for the company to the board, he says the Credo was at its core.

Has having a credo to which everyone subscribes made a difference to J&J? Yes, it's outperformed the S&P 500 pharmaceuticals select industry index and the S&P 500 household and personal products index, and it has raised its dividend for 54 consecutive years.[176] Alan Yu, former managing director of J&J Hong Kong, and an outstanding leader, says "I believe the Credo is one of the reasons why Jim Collins ranks J&J as one of the companies which are 'Built to Last'".

Having people's goals, objectives and behaviour aligned also avoids the vast amount of wasted energy that results when the opposite occurs. Tom Peters says that "Executives spend too much time drafting, wordsmithing, and redrafting vision statements, mission statements, values statements, purpose statements, aspiration statements, and so on. They spend nowhere near enough time trying to align their organizations with the values and visions already in place – when you have superb alignment, a visitor can drop in from another planet and infer the vision without having to read it on paper." [177]

Organizations where common values are held and committed to by everyone, produce better financial results.[178] Longitudinal research has shown that a strong culture, defined as one that engages and motivates employees, generates higher-level performance. Companies without a strong or improving culture tend to become less profitable.[179]

Research done by Bain and Company in 2006 showed that values and culture are recognized as being central to organizational effectiveness.[180] They found that 68% of business executives think that culture and values are the central element in establishing and maintaining competitive advantage. And even more startling, that *81% believe that unless an organization has core values that support a high-performance culture it will never be anything but mediocre.*

Strong cultures provide a level of structure and control that works informally and doesn't involve the restrictive nature of formal structure and bureaucracy. Commonly held values inspire loyalty, get people to want to be part of a team, and motivate them to do what is right, not what is convenient or easiest. As the Bain researchers put it, "people not only know what they should do, they know *why* they should do it".[181]

However, while the data show how much is added when there is a strong culture and its values are uniformly held throughout the organization, many executives pay little more than lip service at best. Lots of organizations have "public" values, by which we mean values that are shown on their websites and in various organizational publications. They're a public relations image "must have", like mission or vision statements, most of which are equally meaningless. In order to find out if an organization's stated values are real or a PR fabrication, the central question is where they originated. Did the organization ask its people what they valued most in terms of their work and relationships, or did someone simply "decide" on the values and publish them? As we all know, the latter is the case in the vast majority of instances.

Organizations with positive cultures and values attract high quality people. Culture is one of the top five things that individuals look at when weighing whether to take a job. It's a highly important element in attracting and retaining talent. Fortune's *100 Best Companies to Work For* all have strong cultures and data shows that they outperform other companies as investments.[182] Organizations with powerful, agreed purpose create emotional commitment. They enable people to get a genuine feeling of making a difference and that's a very powerful motivator.

Leadership behaviour is a critical element in the creation and maintenance of a positive culture. Leaders set an example. You influence people positively or negatively by what you do. If you treat others with respect and make an effort to be supportive and polite, that behaviour tends to be reciprocated.[183] If, on the other hand, you thoughtlessly put people down, are openly critical of others, and so on, research shows that people around you intuitively learn to be selfish and to act in a similar fashion.[184]

Nike is an excellent example of how clear, understood, and accepted, core values and purpose drives excellent performance. Its core promise is "To bring inspiration and innovation to every athlete in the world", and it considers everyone an athlete to some degree or other, the rationale being "if you have a body, you're an athlete". Over the past ten years it has doubled its revenues, doubled its profits and its stock price has gone up five-fold. What a core purpose does is provide the principal criterion for evaluating any and every action. Does what you do support and deliver on the core purpose? If it does, then do it; if it doesn't then don't do it.

If the goal of "bringing inspiration and innovation" sounds a bit vague and difficult to convert to action, here's a simpler example. A hospital we worked with set a core value "to improve patient care", and defined what that meant in measurable terms. It became the principal criterion against which all actions were evaluated. If a suggestion was made to do X, the first question asked was whether doing X would improve patient care and the second question was to what degree. If the answer to the first question wasn't a clear Yes, the suggested was dropped.

Values drive culture

Values and the behaviour that results from them drive culture. Kathleen Redmond has studied and written extensively about culture, and says that a core element of values and culture is the concept of character. She says, "character is much more than what we try to display for others to see. It is who we are when no one is watching". She says a character culture is centred on four central values: respect, integrity, compassion, and courage, and these values "are brought to life in the *behaviours and actions* (italics ours) distinctive to (that culture)". [185]

Research with more than 100 CEOs and 8,000 employees in 84 organizations, both profit and non-profit, shows that character isn't just something "nice", but that organizations led by individuals who clearly demonstrate integrity, responsibility, forgiveness, and compassion outperform those led by individuals who don't by a factor of five.[186] The CEOs who were rated low on integrity, responsibility, forgiveness and compassion were described as "self-focused", and the negative effects of self-focus are hinted at by a somewhat disturbing piece of research about the behaviour of CEOs with MBAs.[187]

The research looked at the performance of CEOs who had been featured on the covers of *Fortune*, *Forbes* and *Businessweek* and their findings showed that those who had MBAs were more likely to engage in behaviours that were of benefit to them but had negative consequences for their companies. In addition, in the three years after they appeared on the cover of one of these publications the market value of their companies declined 20% more than the companies run by non-MBAs. (Full disclosure: The author has an MBA, but he's never been featured on the cover of *Fortune*, *Forbes* or *Businessweek*, and for ratings about his level of self-focus he asks his wife, who is not known for shying away from the truth.)

Is there a best way to go about establishing an organizational culture?

A study into how founders shape the culture and success of their companies identified three organizational blueprints: the engineering blueprint, the star blueprint, and the commitment blueprint.[188] An engineering blueprint organization focuses on hiring people with specific skills central to the company's business. A star blueprint company focuses on poaching the brain power of the best and brightest, on the basis they will be able to acquire the necessary specific skills and expand on them. A commitment blueprint organization emphasises what Steve Jobs talks about in the quote at the beginning of this chapter – cultural fit. The key criterion is a match with the company's values and norms, and a passion for the mission.

The researchers followed the fortunes of about 200 companies through the great internet boom and after the bust in 2000, and the best model proved to be the commitment blueprint. The companies with that focus turned out to be the most resilient - none failed when the dot com bubble burst – and were better performing compared to companies founded on other blueprints.

Does every organization have a set of values?

Jim Collins says that if you scratch the surface and ask people, you will find out what an organization's real values are. Collins says, "I've never encountered an organization, even a global organization composed of people from widely diverse cultures, that could not identify a set of shared values".[189] More commonly, however, organizations have *stated* values that bear no relation to the actual values of the people and groups in the organization. They're mainly there for the decoration or to give a feeling of warmth like Mom, Apple Pie and Santa Claus.

Does everyone in your organization know what its core values are? Do they understand them? Do people demonstrate them in their everyday work? The answer to all of these questions is "Yes". But what they know to be the fact about their organization's values may not be what management says they are. People catch on quickly. They see what gets rewarded and what doesn't. They see who succeeds and who fails. They don't pay any attention to the PR; they just watch what people actually do, and they play along with the game. It doesn't mean they like it, and the statistics about the percentage of employees who are not engaged show how many just put up with it and put in the minimum amount of effort while looking for other opportunities.

Two of Volkswagen's stated values are "Top Performance" and "Customer Orientation". In their elaboration of what they mean by these values they make the following statements: "Top level results can only be achieved if we demand the utmost of ourselves", and "Our internal quality standards are coherently oriented towards the needs, expectations and desires of our customers". It appears however, that for some time they had *not* been demanding the utmost of themselves, and nor had they been focusing on delivering what customers need, expect and desire. The company had installed "defeat software" that activates full emissions controls on diesel engines only during testing but then reduces their effectiveness during normal driving. The result is that cars with these engines can emit nitrogen oxides at up to 40 times the allowable standard".[190]

Why would something like this occur? Why would the biggest carmaker in the world do something so potentially damaging and so flagrantly law breaking? The cost of the action is estimated to end up being around $25 billion.[191] It's unlikely it was a rogue action taken by a small handful of people. But as Robert Armstrong says in *The Financial Times*, "The hard question is not who did it, but why they did it. If a group of people at a company as strong as VW felt that their best option was to go to the dark side, something has to be said about what was going on in their heads or, if you prefer, hearts ... most people and most companies behave honourably not because of the consequences of rule breaking but because they are honourable. If that is true, then we have to assume something went wrong with VW's culture". [192]

You value what's important to you

The Oxford dictionary talks about values being "one's judgement of what is important in life". If you look at the annually published lists of *Best Companies to Work For*, a common element is that their people feel that what they do makes a difference; that it has some impact and importance to the society in which we live. They see what they're doing as being consistent with their fundamental values.

We've been asked a number of times to work with organizations and their values, either to help them gain acceptance at all levels, or sometimes simply to try to measure their application among a small group of senior people. There's certainly nothing wrong with getting the top-level people in the organization "walking the talk" and continuously demonstrating and emphasising the company's values. While an organization's culture is "the way we do things here" and those "things" are determined by what is rewarded and what is not, one assumes that because the people at the top are rewarded the most, what they do is what we should try to emulate in some fashion. You don't have to have an IQ much above room temperature to understand that if you want to advance up the hierarchy, being constantly critical of your boss and acting in a diametrically opposite manner to how she behaves is not likely to improve the probability of your advancement.

But while getting the top handful of people in an organization to subscribe to and demonstrate stated values is a step in the right direction, it's just that – only a step. It doesn't come anywhere near generating the performance levels that are achieved when people at all levels are committed to them.

Extensive research shows that there are two dimensions to expressing the values that determine a culture. We tend to think of culture in terms of shared intellectual values and assumptions – how we think and behave – but there is also an emotional dimension.[193] As a leader you may well believe in certain values and you may try to behave in ways that demonstrate those values, but as we know from the earlier discussion of mirroring, emotional messages are communicated unconsciously and individuals and groups mimic behaviours. So, for instance, if one of the values you hold is openness to, and support of, ideas from all quarters, but when someone comes into your office you remain seated behind your desk, or when you hold a meeting you make sure you sit at the top of the table, the unconscious emotional message sent by those little behaviours is one of dominance. You need to consciously try to model the emotions you want to reinforce in others.

The pressures and difficulties of life outside an organization, let alone inside it, make management of the emotional culture difficult. Who feels light-hearted and happy after a gruelling hour-long commute in heavy traffic, or a long, hot, sweaty ride in a cramped and crowded bus, train or subway? So when you walk into the work place, what's the expression on your face? What emotions are you communicating? People watch you to try to get a sense of how the day is likely to progress. Is this a "keep your head down" day, or is it a day when they feel able to express ideas or make suggestions?

Values and culture can't be imposed

We've been asked a number of times to suggest a set of values for an organization. The request itself tells you everything; this is going to be a purely PR exercise, it's not going to change anyone's behaviour, let alone the behaviour of the people making the request. We try to be as polite as possible in our response, but it's never yes.

You can't "declare" organizational values, you can only discover them. And you can't inject new values into people. Values are not something people "buy in to". A few years ago, we were asked to do some work with an organization concerning their values. We met with a senior executive to talk about what the company wanted us to do and the first thing we asked was what the values were. The executive couldn't name them, but he left his office to get the glossy coloured booklet that listed and described them, a copy of which had been given to everyone in the organization. We waited for about 15 minutes before he returned. He couldn't locate a single copy anywhere. The values had been "invented" by the CEO and introduced to the organization as "this is how we must behave from now on". But you can't tell people in an organization what they value.

Anne Gregory and James Wright make the point that "An organization's character, like those of people, is determined by the values it adopts and pro-actively lives by. No-one imposes these values; they are self-determined."[194] Everyone comes with their own set of values, and a major determinant of whether they are committed to their work is the degree of agreement between those values and the organization's values. When there is a significant clash between these things people leave or become disengaged. Or, in the worst-case scenario, they enter the frightening category of the "actively disengaged" – individuals who aggressively undermine the efforts of their co-workers.

Organizations that are started by individuals with a set of values that they make explicit tend to have those values shared by the people who work in them because the founders did what the quote from Steve Jobs at the beginning of this chapter suggested: they found people who cared about the same things they cared about. A classic example is Bill Hewlett and David Packard, the founders of Hewlett-Packard (HP), who created a very clear and strong company culture that embodied their personal values. That culture remained in place until Hewlett and Packard died. Thomas Watson did the same thing at IBM and his son carried the values forward. The way people are expected to behave in Apple, Google and Amazon are examples of their founders' philosophy and values. But the fact that only 10% of companies are able to sustain these cultures is a dark cloud that is ever-present. HP has moved away from its origins, and the founders' values are forgotten.

How do you embed values?

Given that you can't impose values upon people, it seems pretty clear that the way to start is to find out what they think the organization's values are or should be. When IBM was struggling, CEO Sam Palmisano, took that approach. Using the company's communications technology, he asked every one of IBM's 320,000 employees, spread across 170 countries, to contribute their thoughts on what they thought the company's core values should be. The process generated a set of values to which everyone was committed because they had all been involved and had all had a say.

Start by finding out what the people in an organization think is important – i.e. what they value. Then reinforce and embed those values by rewarding behaviour that demonstrates them. And *don't* reward behaviours that conflicts with them. Values and culture are the glue that holds organizations together. Lou Gerstner, Palmisano's predecessor, is famous for saying "Culture isn't just one aspect of the game, it *is* the game". Peter Drucker put it another way: "*Culture eats strategy for breakfast*".

Is there a downside to culture?

Yes, getting it wrong. Kotter and Heskett studied about 200 companies and showed that when common cultural norms and behaviours don't fit the way the market is moving, they can "systematically undermine an organization's ability to survive and prosper".[195] The organizational world is littered with the corpses or feebly struggling bodies of entities that have failed to recognize the need to change their strong cultures and focus. Some very famous names like Kodak, Polaroid, Nokia, and various print media, spring to mind.

Can you measure values?

Yes. The important thing is to remember that values aren't about what people say, they're about what people *do*. That means that to measure values you have to look at behaviour. Asking people what their values are is a waste of time, even if they're telling the truth. Responses to questions about someone's beliefs and principles tend to be value-laden. Social desirability pushes people to avoid saying what is not considered respectable or desirable. But what people **do**, how they act, will tell you about what they value. It's about their behaviour, and behaviour can be measured because it can be observed.

Key points from this chapter

- Companies that focus on developing a strong set of corporate values over an extended period of time outperform companies that don't by a factor of *five to six times*

- Values are the beginning point and culture is the outcome – the enactment of the values. Culture is "the way people behave from moment to moment without being told"

- Culture is shaped by what gets rewarded and what gets punished or is ignored

- Organizations where common values are held and committed to by everyone, produce better financial results

- 68% of business executives think that culture and values are the central element in establishing and maintaining competitive advantage

- 81% believe that unless an organization has core values that support a high-performance culture it will never be anything but mediocre

- Organizations with positive cultures and values attract high quality people. Culture is one of the top five things that people consider when weighing whether to take a job

- Leadership behaviour is a critical element in the creation and maintenance of a positive culture. Leaders set an example

- You can't "declare" organizational values, you can only discover them. And you can't inject new values into people

7

SECRET 6

Highly Effective Leadership is about making teams productive

"Build for your team a feeling of oneness, of dependence upon one another, and of strength to be derived from unity"

VINCE LOMBARDI

It's a leadership issue. The *New York Times Magazine* reported that increasing numbers of executives believe that profitability rises when workers are persuaded to collaborate more. Effective leadership in teams is important. A review of 93 studies of the relationship between team design features and performance showed that leadership, and particularly empowering leadership, improves team performance.[196] Trust in a team leader has a strong effect on team performance. A study of 30 NCAA basketball teams and the trust the teams had in their coaches showed a highly significant effect on team performance. The two teams with the highest levels of trust in their coach ended up in the top ranks while the team with the lowest level of trust in its coach only won 10% of its conference games.[197]

In his book *Humans are Underrated*, Geoff Colvin makes the point that we are social beings that are hardwired to equate personal relationships with survival.[198] That means we need to work with other people, we need to share ideas, hold conversations, and build relationships. Behaviour – what you do – drives performance. That is as true for teams as it is for individuals. While the makeup of teams and a number of other variables have an effect, it's *how team members act* that is the major factor in determining performance and results.

A survey of team performance studies involving 4,795 teams and 17,279 individuals showed that a central factor of team effectiveness is information sharing.[199] But the *way* information is shared is important. Researchers studied people in different groups doing different types of tasks that all required cooperation, and what they found to be a key factor in team success was *how individuals in the team treated one another.* In the high performing teams, the contributions of team members were relatively equal – they each spoke in approximately the same proportion, as opposed to one or two people doing all the talking. In addition to getting all team members to contribute relatively equally, a second factor that explained high-level performance was that members had high social sensitivity – the ability to read the emotional states of their fellow members and to react with empathy.

These two factors contribute to what social scientists call "psychological safety", defined as "a shared belief held by members of a team that the team is safe for interpersonal risk taking ".[200] It's a feeling of confidence that you can say something or make a suggestion and the team won't ridicule or embarrass you. Amy Edmondson describes it as "a team climate characterized by interpersonal trust and mutual respect in which people are comfortable being themselves".[201] Without it, a team loses out on the skills, knowledge and ideas of some of its team members. You aren't going to put forward an idea if you think you'll be ridiculed.

And there's a third factor that makes teams more effective: having more women on the team. That's because women generally score higher than men on social sensitivity".[202] But men, don't get defensive about it; social sensitivity can be learned.[203] And it has a positive payoff. A survey of employees in 700 companies showed that a caring boss was rated more important than pay.[204] Nobody *has* to be insensitive.

In the very early days of the movement to understand self and the relationship with others, two American psychologists, Joe Luft and Harry Ingham, created what they called the *Johari Window*.[205] It was an attempt to overcome interpersonal problems in groups or teams. Its proposition was that to build trust, people needed to be open about giving and receiving feedback about their behaviour. They needed to divulge some things, but not necessarily everything, about themselves (A tells things about herself to B, C and D). And they should also tell their fellow team members what they observed about them (A tells B, C and D what she has observed that they may, or may not, be conscious of). It provided a framework for giving and receiving feedback and it enabled people to find the distance that made them – and the people they were interacting with – most comfortable.

The philosopher Schopenhauer relates an allegoric tale about the dilemma of hedgehogs in winter. As the temperature gets colder they try to huddle together for warmth but their quills make close contact uncomfortable, so they move apart. But then they get cold again and try to move together, with the same result as before. Eventually they find a distance at which they get some warmth from one another without the experience of being stabbed by the quills of the others. Like hedgehogs, we have a "distance" from others that makes us comfortable. It's a factor that affects interpersonal relationships and therefore team behaviour and performance.

Are teams more productive than individuals?

The prevailing wisdom is that teams are a good thing and teamwork improves performance. Research has shown that effective teams develop a collective intelligence that tends to be greater than the average intelligence of the individuals in the group.[206] But the key word in that sentence is "effective". This doesn't occur in poorly performing teams. It's all about how the team communicates and interacts, because these two things determine the effectiveness of a team more than the knowledge of its individual team members.[207]

But there are two problems with this. Nothing wrong about the research finding; that's established fact. The problems arise because (a) most so-called teams aren't teams, they're just groups of individuals created by the organization chart, and (b) that when they are actual teams they fail to behave appropriately.

There's a vast amount written about teams and team performance but most of it is nonsense. Hopefully this chapter will cut through that and get to the facts about what makes teams work effectively.

Harvard professor Richard Hackman starts off his book *Leading Teams* with a little quiz.[208] The first question he asks is, "When people work together to build a house, will the job probably (a) get done faster, (b) take longer to finish, or (c) not get done? The answer that logic (and popular misconceptions resulting from the vast amount of team-worshipping drivel like "there's no 'I' in team") dictates is: (a) get done faster. But solid research, as well as experience, shows this is simply not true.

Hackman and his colleagues examined 33 different teams, from teams of senior managers to teams of front-line employees, and in widely diverse occupations like prison guards, economic analysts and airline crews, and found that only four or five could be classed as being effective.[209]

Research consistently shows that a great number of teams perform badly. They encounter problems with coordination, with conflicting objectives, with differing motivations. Team leaders come under all kinds of different pressures, trying to balance the various goals and behaviour of members. Trying to set a middle path when disagreements occur tends to make the leader the focus of antagonism from all sides. Nothing unites a group better than a common enemy, and the Shakespearean line in the play *Henry the Fourth, Part 2*, "uneasy lies the head that wears a crown", is not a bad description of the sometimes tenuous nature of team leadership.

An article in the *Harvard Business Review* pointed out that while the time spent in collaborative activities by individuals at all levels in an organization takes up as much as 80 % of the work day, 20-35 % of the value-added collaborations come from only 3-5 % of their members.[210] So high-value productive people have increasing amounts of their time diverted from the specific and critical things they are expected to do on their own, while other individuals spend most of their work day contributing little or nothing.

What is a team?

What constitutes a team? The academic definition is "social entities composed of members with high task interdependency and shared and valued common goals".[211] In everyday language it's *a group of individuals committed to a common goal*. That single criterion, commitment to a common goal, is *the* most critical determinant of success for a high-performing team. Katzenbach and Smith found that "If there is one single criterion that underlies all high performing teams it's the commitment of all of its members to a common goal".[212] Right away you see a big problem. In most cases, they *don't* have a common goal, let alone one to which they are fully committed. They meet to discuss various things, sometimes make decisions, and sometimes translate these decisions into actions. They attempt, largely unsuccessfully, to keep emotional and inter-personal issues at bay. And generally speaking their performance is poor.[213]

"Keeping emotional and inter-personal issues largely at bay" is another key issue in poor team performance. Manfred Kets de Vries, a distinguished management expert, asks the question, "Why do so many teams fail to live up to their promise?" And his response is, "The answer lies in the obstinate belief that human beings are rational entities".[214] They aren't. Their behaviour has a large emotional content. Kets de Vries says that it is also affected by various unconscious forces. These rise up from time to time and cause waves that have to be dealt with. Research shows that teams in which the members are open minded and emotionally stable perform better than those who are unable to understand emotions well. [215]

A rational entity that takes a purely logical approach to problems is unable to manage the essential interpersonal elements of team interaction and functioning. David Kirk, former New Zealand All Blacks Rugby team captain, says "The key competence for world-class teams is the ability to recognize, face, and tackle interpersonal issues promptly".[216] Teams are all about interpersonal relationships and these are driven more by emotion than logic. Research also shows that "as conflict intensifies and arousal increases, cognitive load increases, which interferes with cognitive flexibility and creative thinking".[217] In other words, when emotions run high, people are less able to adjust their thinking to deal with the situation.

If you believe that people are rational entities, then it's logical to assume that a group of people should have more power than an individual because the power of the individuals becomes additive. However, somewhat off-beat research studying the energy of people pulling on a rope was done in the early 1900s by Maximilien Ringelmann. It showed that as more people were added to pull on a rope, each individual exerted less energy. The "Ringelmann Effect" shows up in teams or groups where adding individuals to the team ends up decreasing individual effort and coordination.

Situational elements affecting team performance

There are, of course, lots of teams that do perform well and do produce value-adding results. One of the more innovative studies of team behaviour, conducted by Manfred Kets de Vries, was about highly effective pygmy groups.[218]

There are 10 or so small pygmy tribal groups living in the Congo-Zaire basin. They are essentially foraging groups whose habitat is hostile and difficult. *When both the cost of failure and the reward for success are high, and when both of these are linked to cooperative effort, there is a compelling need to create an effective team.* For the Congo pygmies, effective teamwork is critical – team success is life, and team failure is death. De Vries found that the groups were characterised by seven characteristics. They:

- Demonstrate a high level of respect and trust for one another
- Are supportive and protective of one another

- Share common goals
- Hold common values
- View the individual as less important than the group
- Support completely open communication
- Move leadership between individuals depending on the situation

If you look through this list, you see that it conforms to what much of the research we've talked about shows to be true – mutual respect and support, open and balanced communication, shared leadership and a common focus. Sberbank, Russia's biggest bank, has as a central pillar of its culture the statement "I am a leader" that refers to everyone at all levels. But Sberbank also recognizes the critical importance of working cooperatively, and the second pillar of the culture is "We are the team".[219]

When a team is given clear, unambiguous and totally uncompromising performance demands, there is no back door; they either have to deliver or fold. And to deliver they have to become a real team. Their feet are put to the fire of actual, no-nonsense, no-games performance demands.

Size does matter

We're constantly asked whether team size makes a difference. The generally agreed qualifier on team effectiveness is that an effective operating team must also be small.

The upper size range tends to be no more than ten people and there seems to be a consensus among researchers that five to eight works best. Evan Wittenberg, the director of the Wharton School of Business Graduate Leadership Program says that although the research on optimal team size is "not conclusive, it does tend to fall into the five to twelve range, though some say five to nine is best, and the number six has come up a few times".[220]

The Wharton School of Business assigns individuals to teams that work together during the MBA programme. But Wharton doesn't simply allocate people to a team and let them get on with it. Before they begin to work together, the MBA students have to agree their team goals, their team principles and values, and their team behaviour norms – how they will operate, who will do what, what's acceptable and what's unacceptable behaviour. In other words, they set the groundwork for the establishment of a high level of interdependency. And they establish the foundation on which the team can begin to overcome what Kets de Vries identifies as the major stumbling block to effective team operation, - the assumption that all the members will act purely rationally.

The Roman army organized men who lived together, ate together, etc., in groups of eight. In a fighting situation, much as in fluid sports situations, it is important, without having to look around directly for them, to know where your teammates are and what they're likely to be doing. Small teams of people can do that, large groups can't. The issue is interdependency. How can a private soldier feel accountable for the performance of another soldier who, while perhaps belonging to the same regiment, may be in a completely different battalion, company or platoon?

But apart from agreeing goals, values and behaviour norms for the team, there is a surprising process element that adds signifi-cantly to team productivity. It's structured and mandatory time off. Having demonstrated with in-company research that this results in greater productivity, thousands of consultant teams in the Boston Consulting Group arrange to spend time out of the office, completely divorced from work and communications from work. Harvard professor Leslie Perlow, who introduced this process to BCG, says

"Teams that set a goal of structured time off – and crucially, meet regularly to discuss how they'll work together to ensure that every member takes it – have more open dialogue, (and) engage in more experimentation and innovation."[221]

Leadership in teams

Whoever assumes responsibility for satisfying a team's needs can be viewed as taking on a team leadership role. Leadership plays a significant role in high performance teams, but leaders would be well advised to heed one of the central principles of Behaviour Kinetics: there is a very strong *Ask Them* element to high performance teams. [222] Everyone needs to have ownership; *Tell Them* doesn't give ownership. Goals have to be shared, not dictated. Individuals who, to paraphrase the Star Trek mission statement, boldly go where the team has not gone before – and perhaps doesn't want to go – destroy team effectiveness rather than creating it. Directive, authoritative leaders have to be careful not to overplay their hand. While teams value having a clear direction and need someone to provide the initiative and stimulus to set the direction, individual members also want to be made part of the input, the discussion and the decision-making process.

Leaders are always role models of one kind or another. But leaders in high performance teams have to achieve a delicate balance between modelling a role that the team will engage and follow, and inadvertently projecting a model which is consistently too far out in front of the team. Everyone understands the unique role of the leader and they don't expect him or her to be able to excel at everything. What they do expect is that the leader will maintain a good grasp of the overall working of the team and enable each member to fulfil their role and contribute their best. Being the star performer who is always in front acting as the lead dog, and who is always "helping" team members who are not doing what the he or she expects, gets in the way of team performance. And taking all the challenging and rewarding tasks yourself and leaving the less attractive work to the other members of the team isn't leadership either, it's egotism.

The leadership style that is most effective for creating high performance teams is a balance of three main things: taking initiative and setting an example, listening to people's input and ideas, and employing full-strength delegation – i.e. being confident in giving tasks to people and not interfering with them. This is a very difficult behavioural combination to master and we have found it to be relatively rare (slightly less than 20%) among the many thousands of managers we have studied and worked with.

Being an "Ask Them" leader, rather than a "Tell Them" one, doesn't mean sitting back and never putting forward any ideas or suggestions yourself. The role of the leader is to lead and that means that she or he has to make some decisions about what others should be doing and what the team should be doing. *There is a real, but subtle, difference between initiating goals and objectives and involving people in the process at crucial points.* Effective team leadership requires a fine balance between direction and guidance and consultation, between making critical decisions and letting others make them, and between control and delegation. Erring too much on the side of control and direction undermines innovation, involvement and commitment, but erring too much on the other side and demonstrating no direction, no initiative and no willingness to make hard decisions removes the focus on performance and creates confusion and de-motivation.

Role and skill flexibility

One characteristic of high performance teams is the ability to allow and support members to flex their roles and responsibilities to deal with responsibility gaps and overlaps to everyone's satisfaction. One of the problems that haunts ineffective teams is the issue of who is responsible for what. There are often conflicts over whether A or B is responsible for something, or over how a joint responsibility between B and C is to be dealt with, or how to deal with the situation where there is a team responsibility for something but nobody in the team is taking personal responsibility. Low performance teams are plagued with responsibility overlaps and underlaps. Problems remain hidden and often fester and grow when surfacing them would allow them to be dealt with easily.

Role flexibility is an important ingredient in effective group performance. By role flexibility we mean that the group leadership allows and enables individuals to move into roles where they can add most value. Too often people get pigeonholed. In one multi-national with which we were familiar, once an individual entered a specific function – finance, marketing, sales, production, IT, etc. – they were unable to move to another one. This is not an exaggeration. Over a period of three years of study of this company, in no case were we ever able to observe a person successfully managing to move from a role in one business function to a role in another function. Without exception when they made the move they either left the company or were fired within six months. This was silo management at its most extreme and the company suffered as a result of it.

The absolute opposite of this situation is provided by another multi-national company we worked with that adopted a policy of offering all its senior and middle managers the opportunity to decide where they thought they could add most value to the company, and supporting the role changes they suggested. Over the three years during which we worked with them they tripled their revenues.

In teams where roles are either too rigidly defined, or poorly defined, problems occur. Rigid role definition stifles individuals' ability to acquire new skills and limits the team's capability to deal with changing situations. Poor, unclear role definition often leads to problems of role conflict as two or more people claim responsibility for the same things.

A team is created when you have:

- A small group of people
- Who have complementary skills and experience
- Who are all deeply committed to a common purpose and goal
- Who accept working by a clear set of rules
- Who trust one another to (a) do as they say and (b) do what they can to help every other member of the team, and
- Who accept mutual responsibility for outcomes – "We're all in this together. If I fail, we all fail; if you fail we all fail; if we succeed everyone succeeds." The Three Musketeers motto is the right one: "One for all and all for one"

High-performance teams display a common set of behaviours

We've been researching team behaviour for what is approaching fifty years, and we've identified eleven behaviours that determine the effectiveness of work teams.

1. Create a shared commitment to what has to be done [223] [224]

2. Constantly suggest ideas to increase effectiveness [225]

3. Make sure people are treated with respect [226]

4. Work for a win-win resolution to conflicts [227] [228]

5. Face up to and deal with demanding situations [229]

6. Help people to learn from their mistakes [230]

7. State views frankly and openly [231]

8. Hold people accountable for their commitments [232]

9. Give and accept open and frank feedback [233]

10. Encourage contributions from everyone [234]

11. Set clear priorities and stick with them [235]

These are all behaviours that can be observed and measured. We use diagnostic instruments to do that, but there are other ways. The important thing to remember is the management maxim "what gets measured gets done". Keeping all team members focused on demonstrating the essential core behaviours for effective performance is critical. One of the ways to do that is to institute the discipline of taking the last 5 minutes of every meeting to ask whether the team has done these eleven things.

What are the benefits of working in a team?

A *Forbes* article looks at the issue from the opposite perspective: what are the downsides of working alone? [236] The author lists the following reasons, but since he's someone who enjoys working in teams one might argue that he *would* think these things are true, wouldn't he?

- Working alone makes it harder to get early and continual feedback
- Working alone reduces learning

- Working on a team increases accountability

- Slower project momentum from working alone reduces morale

- The lows of a project are more demoralizing when working alone

- The highs of a project are more motivating when working as a team

- Working in a team increases the bus factor

What's "the bus factor"? The more people you have on a team, the lower the probability of failure if one or more gets run over by a bus

Key points from this chapter

A high-performing team is created when you have:

- A small group of people

- Who have complementary skills and experience

- Who are all deeply committed to a common purpose and goal

- Who accept working by a clear set of rules

- Who trust one another to (a) do as they say and (b) do what they can to help every other member of the team, and who accept mutual responsibility for outcomes – "We're all in this together. If I fail, we all fail; if you fail we all fail; if we succeed everyone succeeds." The Three Musketeers motto is the right one: "One for all and all for one"

- High-performance teams:

    - Create a shared commitment to what has to be done

    - Constantly suggest ideas to increase effectiveness

    - Make sure people are treated with respect

    - Work for a win-win resolution to conflicts

    - Face up to and deal with demanding situations

    - Help people to learn from their mistakes

    - State views frankly and openly

    - Hold people accountable for their commitments

    - Give and accept open and frank feedback

    - Encourage contributions from everyone

    - Set clear priorities and stick with them

8

SECRET 7

Highly Effective Leadership is about how you react to pressure and stress

---

Behaviour is a mirror in which everyone displays his own image

JOHANN WOLFGANG VON GOETHE

The UK Health and Safety Executive defines stress this way: "*Stress is the reaction people have to excessive pressures or other types of demands placed upon them. It arises when they worry that they can't cope*". That's a leadership issue. If leaders put people in situations where they feel they have no control, where they don't think they can make a contribution, and where they feel they aren't valued, stress is the result. Feelings of helplessness can sometimes lead to unfortunate events. A bumper sticker's dark humour expresses this quite pithily: "All stressed out and nobody to choke".

Researchers investigating the costs of stress to business in the United States say that while overall mortality and health spending on stress in the United States is not specifically recorded, they estimate it results in more than 120,000 deaths per year and approximately 5-8% of annual healthcare costs.[237] *Forbes* estimates the cost in dollar terms as being as high as $190 billion.[238]

In Britain, the Health and Safety Executive says that stress accounted for 37% of all work related ill health cases and 45% of all working days lost due to ill health in 2015/16. And it says that the total number of working days lost due to stress over that period was 11.7 million days.[239] Stress is a major issue, and flagging and dealing with it before it wreaks its damage is a duty which is unfortunately neglected by the vast majority of organizations both in the public and private sector. There are visible behavioural signs of stress but we hope it's never as bad as this definition by some wag: "Stress is when you wake up screaming and you realise that you haven't fallen asleep yet".

Studying behaviour in the workplace over the years we have made some interesting discoveries. We discovered, as we said earlier, that certain actions *accelerate* an organization's performance and other actions *sustain* it. But we also observed and measured a third set of behaviours. These are destructive actions that waste energy and get in the way of productivity, efficiency and effectiveness. We call them *performance hindering behaviours*, and research shows that the negative effect of these behaviours is **five times greater** than the positive effect of accelerating or sustaining actions.[240] People remember negative interactions with their boss more often, in more detail, and in more intensity, than they do positive ones.[241]

These behaviours also have a disastrous physical effect. A 20-year study involving 6,000 civil servants in Britain showed that when managers treated their people badly, criticised them unfairly, and didn't give them recognition or praise for good work, they suffered a significantly greater incidence of coronary heart disease.[242]

The brain is hyper-sensitive to this type of behaviour, even when it's not experienced directly. Simply witnessing negative behaviour affects the observers' performance.[243] It activates a node in the brain and that, in turn, activates nearby nodes and spreads across the neutral network.[244] The result is that the behaviour is "experienced" across a wider audience than just its direct recipient(s).[245]

Defensive-aggressive behaviour, or as researcher Christine Porath calls it, "incivil behaviour" – rudeness, bullying, demeaning, etc. – is the type of performance hindering behaviour that gets the most attention, and its consequences can be dramatic. For instance, a survey of more than 4,000 doctors, nurses and hospital workers found abusive, insulting, and condescending behaviours were connected to medical errors, *and patient deaths*.[246] A second hospital study of 4,500 doctors and nurses revealed that 71% of the respondents linked insulting, condescending and rude behaviour to medical errors they had observed, and 27%" tied the behaviour to fatalities.[247]

In an experiment, 24 medical teams were invited to a training workshop in which they engaged in a simulation treating a premature infant whose condition deteriorated suddenly due to intestinal illness. The teams had to identify the condition and provide appropriate treatment. Their performance was observed remotely via video by an individual they were told was an expert. For half the teams the "expert" (a researcher) provided no comment other than to speak about the importance of training using simulations, while the other half were given insulting comments about their performance and poor medical care. These latter teams performed worse on all diagnostic and procedural measures, shared less information, and asked for less help from teammates, resulting in significantly diminishing the chances of survival of the (simulated) infant.[248]

But there are other types of performance hindering behaviours that can have equally devastating effects. They are conflict avoidance and responsibility avoidance. Using the hospital environment as an example again, conflict avoidance – not challenging bad procedures or bad decisions – also causes medical errors and patient deaths. And so does responsibility avoidance. These actions are less visible than abusive, shouting, bullying, intimidating behaviour, and they are more easily swept under the carpet, but in our many years of working with hospitals around the world we've seen instance after instance where their consequences were highly damaging.

Defensive-aggressive behaviour

Let's start with defensive-aggressive actions because they're the performance hindering behaviours with which most people are familiar.

We know that effective behaviour is determined by the requirements of the job. Is there any job that requires negative, performance hindering actions? *No.* Is there any kind of sound rationale for doing these things? *No.* In fact, studies at the Center for Creative Leadership show that *the number one characteristic of executives who fail is an aggressive, bullying, insensitive style.*

Add to that the fact that people who *don't* behave this way, and whose behaviour is positive and pleasant, are twice as likely to be seen as leaders. In fact, studies show that simply by listening, smiling and saying thank you, people were seen to be 27% warmer, 22% more civil, and 13% more competent.[249] And they displayed better performance. Research in 2015 concluded "The more the individual was perceived as civil by others in his or her network, the better his or her performance".[250]

Christine Porath says that over 20 years of surveying thousands of people at work she has found that 98% have experienced defensive-aggressive behaviour and 99% have witnessed it, and that seeing or experiencing this behaviour impairs short-term memory and cognitive ability. [251] She says half the people surveyed said they were treated badly at least once a week, and she adds, "for every eight people who report working in an incivil environment, approximately one leaves as a result".

She gives examples of some of these types of incivil behaviours: "walking away during a conversation (rudely indicating) lost interest; answering calls in the middle of meetings without leaving the room; openly mocking people by pointing out their flaws or personality quirks in front of others; ... taking credit for wins, but pointing the finger at others when problems arise".[252]

Research by Porath and Amir Erez leads them to conclude "that even when the target of rudeness does not exact retribution, performance plummets, whether measured using cognitive or creative tasks, or in terms of helpfulness. What's more, witnesses are affected in similar ways. Rudeness even primes dysfunctional behaviour and aggressive thoughts. Findings suggest that rudeness can tarnish a culture – it takes a toll on people and society in multiple ways".[253] [254]

When we talk about the dynamics of defensive-aggressive behaviour we are talking about what is termed *social-evaluative threat*. It is the concern we all have for how others think of us and evaluate us. Its results are that people feel demeaned, or ashamed, or rejected. And research shows it has physical consequences as well as psychological ones.[255] It triggers large bursts of cortisol and pro-inflammatory cytokine. At high levels, cortisol and adrenaline interfere with the functioning of the brain, shrinking cells and affecting decision making.

They also affect self-awareness, resulting in people doing and saying things they wouldn't do or say normally. In addition, they heighten self-conscious emotions, and the combination of the heightened emotion plus high levels of cortisol and adrenaline has a negative effect on the immune system, which helps to explain why people who are bullied and made to feel demeaned can become ill. If that wasn't bad enough, research also shows that the greatest cause of stress for people occurs when they feel they are under social-evaluative threat and are also in situations where they have little or no control over things.[256]

The concept of stress in humans was identified in 1936 by Hans Selye with his creation of the model, *The General Adaptive Syndrome,* which explains the stress response. As Selye described it, "Every stress leaves an indelible scar, and the organism pays for its survival after a stressful situation by becoming a little older".[257] Selye was understating things. Stress can have quite dramatic consequences. The fact is that intense or prolonged stress impairs the working of the pre-frontal cortex (PFC) which runs cognitive abilities, drives creativity and imagination, and enables sensible decision-making. The longer stress persists the greater the damage to cognitive abilities. Even quite mild uncontrollable stress causes a significant loss of pre frontal cognitive abilities.[258] Walter Mischel says "The architecture of the brain is literally remodeled under chronic stress".[259]

Robert Sutton, a professor at Stanford, says that people who demonstrate this aggressive, bullying behaviour aim it at people who are *less* powerful rather than at people who are more powerful. He's scathing about the kind of people who behave like this, and comments that "the difference between how a person treats the powerless versus the powerful is as good a measure of human character as I know".[260]

Sutton has two tests of whether someone is a bully:

1. After talking to the person, do you "feel oppressed, humiliated, de-energised, or belittled"? And specifically do you feel worse about yourself?

2. Does the person who indulges in this behaviour "aim his or her venom at people who are less powerful rather than at people who are more powerful"?

Here's an example of highly destructive defensive-aggressive behaviour that meets Sutton's criteria.

> When meeting with her boss, ostensibly to write a recruitment advertisement, the individual described the process as: "He would 'write' it while screaming at me, quite literally screaming, as in you could hear him a city block away and through three concrete slabs. I would be called an idiot, a moron, clueless, cursed at, insulted, demeaned, and physically threatened at each 'meeting.' At the end of the meeting I would have a page of scrawled, nearly impossible to read sentence fragments which he would demand be published as is, no editing. So I would. Once published, like clockwork, I would get a phone call or a follow up meeting with this same moron, screaming at me, insulting me, and threatening me still more, all because he didn't like the ad that HE wrote and demanded I post without any editing" [261]

And another example, with the behaviour this time being driven by a feeling of threat from a subordinate who was promoted:

> "I had a good working relationship with my boss. In the fifth year, when I was promoted, my boss started to change; he would make mean remarks concerning my work in front of colleagues; he started to discriminate against me when calling for meetings, and started to accuse me of things I hadn't done. When I tried to have a discussion with him he denied that anything was the matter and intensified his attacks to the extent of removing my parking and invading my privacy by checking my call records. He then made allegations against me of poor performance and demanded that I sign a performance improvement plan".[262]

This type of behaviour is often a reaction to threatened self-esteem and self-concept. And the reason that it's generally directed to those of lower status and power, as the examples show, is that the person exhibiting the behaviour somehow feels threatened by the individual or group to whom they direct the behaviour.

You may see these as extreme examples, but the fact is that this type of behaviour, albeit generally in a less overtly brutal form, is exhibited by people in leadership roles all the time. A study of employees in US organizations showed that 10% reported witnessing instances of bullying, demeaning and offensive behaviour in their workplaces *every day*, while 20% were targets at least once a week.[263]

A research paper showed that: "more than half the targets (of incivil behaviour) waste work time worrying about the incident or planning how to deal with or avert future interactions with the instigator. Nearly 40% reduced their commitment to the organization; 20% told us that they reduced their work effort intentionally as a result of the incivility, and 10% of targets said that they deliberately cut back the amount of time they spent at work".[264]

The behaviour also has an unfortunate chain effect. Research published in the journal *Personnel Psychology* concluded, "Abusive manager behaviour is positively related to abusive supervisor behaviour which, in turn, is positively related to work group interpersonal deviance" [265] What starts at the top goes right down through the organization and creates a toxic culture.

Defensive-Aggressive behaviour involves directing anger at people, pressuring them, belittling them, bullying them. It's a short-term emotional release which flares up quickly and can subside just as quickly. When the outcome of something has a bearing on your reputation, standing, authority, credibility or power base, it's easy to fall into the trap of defensive behaviour. Look behind defensive-aggressive behaviour and you'll often find a fear of failure, or a perceived threat to self-perception. As the American philosopher Eric Hoffer put it, "rudeness is the weak man's imitation of strength".

Sometimes it's very difficult to control the impulse to give vent to anger. Something that has annoyed you triggers stimuli in the hippocampus and amygdala which form emotionally charged memories that linger and fester as you continue to revisit them. As you experience a series of annoying or frustrating incidents over which you have little or no control, the anger builds and then something happens that pushes you over the limit. It can be something small to which you wouldn't normally react, but when your anger has built up without an outlet, it seeks the first possible one in order to release the cognitive pressure. It's called displacement, but no matter what it's called, someone, or something, gets an undeserved earful.

Unfortunately, people who exhibit repetitive defensive-aggressive behaviour demonstrate low sensitivity to others, and they often move from one situation to another oblivious to the pain, chaos and indignity created in their wake. While managers who lose their temper and tear a strip off subordinates may feel better for it, the subordinates are unlikely to be sympathetic and understanding. Rather, they find this type of behaviour upsetting, embarrassing, belittling and insulting. They see the manager as immature and undisciplined – and they're right. Defensive-aggressive behaviour may massage the perpetrator's emotions fleetingly, but it inflicts longer term bruising on its recipients and it creates a huge amount of wasted energy.

Defensive-aggressive behaviour may be understandable but that doesn't make it acceptable. It's an immature reaction and if you want to be a good performer and show real leadership then you have to resist engaging in it.

Two essential points

First, Freud said – but he was wrong – that holding back anger simply built up pressure in the system and that it was best to release the pressure by venting the anger. So people rationalise venting anger as being in some sense "good for you". But Adam Grant, in his book *Originals*, observes that "Venting doesn't extinguish the flame of anger; it feeds it. When we vent our anger, we put a lead foot on the gas pedal of the go system, attacking the target who enraged us."[266]

And there is solid research that proves this. Research done by Brad Bushman shows that venting anger: *makes you angrier and more aggressive.*[267] You may think you feel good when you let it all out, but that's pure rationalisation; you're actually making things worse for yourself. Instead of letting anger build up, try, each time something annoys or frustrates you, to step back and, at least figuratively, as Thomas Jefferson suggested, count to 100 and calm yourself. It ain't easy, but it's worth trying. The Monty Python song, *Always Look on the Bright Side of Life*, has a lot to be said for it.

The second thing to remember about defensive-aggressive behaviour is that, like all performance hindering behaviour, it can be changed. You *can* stop reacting to things defensively. You *don't* have to vent your anger at people. You *don't* have to bully and pressure people. You *don't* have to demean, threaten or belittle them. When you do these things it's not to benefit others, it's purely to give yourself the illusion of being strong. As another great American statesman, Benjamin Franklin, observed, "Anger is never without a reason, but seldom a good one".

Conflict avoidance

Aggressive, bullying, insensitive, incivil actions aren't the only type of behaviour that hinders performance. A survey of 656 people in 2010 concluded that by engaging in conflict avoidance, individuals in organizations waste the equivalent of an eight-hour working day and cost about $1500.[268] But conflict avoidance doesn't just waste time; it spreads its effects and creates more conflict. Dr Glenn Marron says, "If you're a conflict avoider, then, by definition, you're a conflict creator ... think of it as setting a fire and then running, leaving it to others to clean up".[269]

The objective of conflict avoidance is to avoid getting people upset at you, or challenging you, or getting you involved in an argument. But false agreement is clearly a negative behaviour and people recognize it as such. Dr Marron says that if you're a conflict avoider, the reactions of people towards your behaviour will be stronger than they would have been if you'd been honest and stated your views. Interestingly, research shows that individuals who have a high level of emotional intelligence tend not to avoid conflict, but instead seek to discuss the issues and work towards a collaborative solution to the dispute.[270]

People who engage in conflict avoidance behaviour try to avoid challenging others' opinions, avoid giving negative feedback, avoid being controversial, avoid giving constructive criticism, avoid voicing opposing views, avoid risk, and generally attempt to indicate agreement to points put forward or decisions made by others, regardless of how they personally feel about them. This behaviour can be extremely frustrating for people who work with them. They never feel that they really know where the conflict avoider stands on issues. They're not sure, when the person states an opinion or appears to make a decision, whether it's a real decision or a real opinion. They don't trust the feedback they get, if any. They feel let down. As Dr Martin Luther King said, "A time comes when silence is betrayal".

Conflict avoidance has a correlation with stress and ill-health.[271] A study has shown that people who adopt avoidance as a way of dealing with conflict experience higher levels of stress and exhaustion, and poor general health, and have a higher number of sickness days than those who resolve the conflict through discussion.[272] Another study showed that avoidance behaviour also resulted in lower mental health scores for those who used escape–avoidance.[273]

These studies, of course, provide further confirmation that behaviour is driven by the situation. For instance, nurses show a strong preference not to confront conflict directly, while nursing managers are less likely to shy away from direct confrontation, but still show a preference for not doing so.[274] Hospitals have what can be described as marked "status schisms", where there is a clearly understood demarcation between the status of one group and another. The armed forces are an example of formal status schisms in the structure – officers, non-commissioned officers, other ranks. In hospitals, the physicians occupy the top status and power layer, and they tend to maintain a clear gap between themselves and the next level. Then come the nurses, but within that population, there is once again a significant status break between nursing managers and staff nurses. And there are further layers of types of nursing qualifications and levels of trainee nurses.

Without conflicting views and opinions, and without the ability to engage and discuss them and come to an agreement of some kind, progress is next to impossible. Conflict avoidance has a slow burn and it spreads a poison which can be difficult to eradicate.

Responsibility avoidance

At any level, avoiding responsibility is damaging. For leaders it borders on the criminal. It manifests itself in a variety of ways – moving actions down the priority ranking and "never getting around to them", avoiding putting structure and processes in place, continuously shifting from one set of tasks to another, side-stepping potentially risky decisions or actions, and so on, and it always has a negative effect on performance.[275]

A great deal of performance hindering behaviour results from the frustration of being robbed of self-worth, and that's what bad leaders do to people. There is a high correlation between superiors who engage in defensive-aggressive behaviour – bullying, pressuring, criticizing – and subordinates who become skilled at getting out of the way. People who are berated, belittled, cowed, and given no recognition for success, but are reprimanded for mistakes, learn to avoid taking any responsibility if at all possible. It's a perfectly logical decision.[276] It may take some animals repeated pain to learn not to do something, but humans generally tend to learn quicker.

And they tend to have longer memories. "Once bitten, twice shy" is something managers should think about when they deal badly with colleagues and subordinates.

While leaders who turn their back on difficult situations may allay some of their own anxieties and frustrations, they pass them on to others. If someone avoids responsibility, someone else has to accept it. The phrase "passing the buck" implies that someone "catches the buck". It is important to recognize that problems won't go away on their own. Ostrich-like behaviour doesn't solve problems; it simply removes them from sight temporarily.

A *Harvard Business Review* article, "How Damaging is a Bad Boss Exactly?" shows a straight-line correlation between engagement of employees and leader effectiveness – the higher the level of engagement the greater the effectiveness of a leader, and the lower the level of engagement, the poorer the effectiveness.[277] Engagement is about positive behaviour towards people - involvement, respect, recognition and reinforcing people's self-esteem. The number one factor that drives employee engagement is whether managers are genuinely interested in their people's well-being, and that they demonstrate it.[278] Hindering behaviour is the opposite; it's about aggression, bullying, belittling, conflict avoidance, responsibility avoidance, and disengagement.

Hindering behaviour is contagious

Unfortunately, the issue of performance hindering behaviour isn't just about negatively affecting the performance of one or two individuals, the real problem is that when people interact with someone who is doing these types of things they start to behave in a negative fashion themselves.[279] They either become angry, antagonistic and resentful, or they back away from conflict, responsibility and involvement and, as Peter Drucker described it, "retire on the job". Having been affected by the negative actions of one individual they find themselves engaging in reciprocal negative behaviour and passing it on to others. They haven't simply become infected; they've become infec*tious*. Christine Porath, who has probably done more research on this type of behaviour than anyone, says, "In truth, incivility is a virus that spreads, making the lives of everyone exposed to it more difficult".[280] And it's not just incivility that's viral, it's also conflict avoidance and responsibility avoidance.

Fear, uncertainty and frustration are powerful negative motivators. A research study of 260 managers in the US found that more than 44% of conflict avoidance behaviours and responsibility avoidance behaviours resulted from fear of repercussion. Another 17% of these behaviours was due to frustration – "nothing will change as a result of anything I do".[281]

These are worrying statistics. While part of this feeling of insecurity (which almost always translates itself into some form of energy-wasting, hindering behaviour) may be due to the uncertainties of change, the majority is due to bad leadership. If your boss won't be honest about plans for change, won't show clear support for you, won't make a decision, won't set or agree clear objectives for you, won't stand by an agreement, intimidates you or embarrasses you in public, how "secure" do you think you're going to feel? And if you don't feel overly secure, how engaged and proactive are you going to be? How much initiative are you likely to take? How much change are you likely to drive? How much vision and excitement are you likely to bring to your job?

While engaging in hindering behaviour always has negative consequences, research indicates that this is magnified if the behaviour is inconsistent. A study done at Michigan State University looked at the effects of bosses who act one way some of the time and act differently at other times.[282] Specifically they looked at the effects of individuals demonstrating positive behaviour at one moment and negative behaviour the next. The study involved 161 individuals divided into three groups, one of which received consistently favourable comments on their performance, one of which received consistently unfavourable comments, and a third group who got a mix of favourable and unfavourable comments. The first group (consistently favourable comments) showed the lowest stress, the second group (consistently unfavourable comments) showed the second lowest stress levels, but the third group (a random mix between favourable and unfavourable comments) showed the highest levels of stress.

How to deal with performance hindering behaviour

In dealing with performance hindering behaviour – either yours or someone else's – it's important to remember that it *is **not** driven by personality, it is the product of forces external to the individual. It is caused by something happening to you or them and if that can be identified and dealt with the behaviour will stop.*

A warning: Christine Porath says that she has found that 85% of those who choose confrontation with an incivil boss make things worse.[283] She suggests that a better way is to try to make yourself impervious to it. And to focus on the positive aspects of yourself, getting the negative stuff out of your mind and becoming more resilient. Always remember Eleanor Roosevelt's advice: "No one can make you feel inferior without your consent".

Once you recognize how you react to various things you can begin to think about how to deal with them. Can you moderate your reaction to these things? For instance, if you get irritable and somewhat aggressive when you are pressured to meet deadlines, is there something you can do to overcome this? Could you work out how to plan a little better or get started on things earlier? Or could you set firm goals and priorities and resist being pulled away from them and being drawn into other people's crises?

If you want to decrease your performance hindering behaviours, the first step in the process is to identify the specific things you do – the specific ways you duck conflict, avoid responsibility, or vent your frustration. You can do this by thinking about your recent behaviour. Or you can ask someone close to you about what they see you doing.

How to change your behaviour

You can't change your behaviour until you know exactly what you're doing now. And you won't change your behaviour unless you acknowledge and accept what you're doing. Acceptance and understanding of a situation are prerequisites to being able to decide what to do about it. The steps are simple:

1. **Identify the behaviour** – Ask someone who knows you well, and whom you trust, to tell you what you do, and when. The last bit, when, is very important because it helps you with step three in this process.

2. **Acknowledge it** – The first step in the AA program is acknowledgment. You can't, and won't, deal with something unless you acknowledge it as a reality. It's useful to get some confirming data to help you accept what you're doing.

3. **Determine the cause** – Think about when you do these things and what has occurred just prior to the behaviour.

Performance hindering behaviours are reactions to things that frustrate, annoy, pressure, question or undermine self-confidence and self-esteem, create uncertainty, and so on.

4. **Deal with the cause** – If you can get rid of the cause then you will get rid of the reaction. That's what doctors do for their patients. They identify what's causing the illness and do something that gets rid of it.

5. **If you can't get rid of the cause, then change the way you react to it** – That's not always easy. Emotions are powerful things. But you *can* control them if you make an effort. Viktor Frankl, neurologist, psychiatrist, and holocaust survivor said, "When we are no longer able to change a situation, we are challenged to change ourselves".[284]

The bottom line is this: Exhibiting hindering behaviour is understandable; continuing it after you've been made aware of it is unforgivable. Using the excuse "I can't help it because it's just my personality" doesn't cut it. The response to anyone who says that is "Grow up".

Key points from this chapter

- The negative effect of performance hindering behaviours is *five times greater* than the positive effect of accelerating or sustaining actions

- When leaders treat their people badly, criticise them unfairly, and don't give them recognition or praise for good work, the people suffer a significantly greater incidence of coronary heart disease

- Negative behaviour is contagious. It only has to be witnessed to have a harmful effect

- One in every eight people who report working in an incivil environment leaves as a result

- Social-evaluative threat – the concern we have for how others think of us and evaluate us – is a major driver of stress and negative behaviour

- At high or sustained levels, the stress produced by social-evaluative threat can have physical consequences, shrinking braincells and affecting decision making

- It also diminishes self-awareness, heightens emotions, and can have a negative effect on the immune system

- The longer stress persists the greater the damage to cognitive abilities

- Venting anger doesn't relieve you of the pressure and make you calmer, it makes you angrier and more aggressive

- if you're a conflict avoider, the reactions of people towards your behaviour will be stronger than they would have been if you'd been honest and stated your views

- People who adopt avoidance as a way of dealing with conflict experience higher levels of stress and exhaustion, and poor general health, and have a higher number of sickness days than those who resolve the conflict through discussion

- Performance hindering, negative behaviour is not driven by personality, it is driven by forces external to the individual. It is caused by something happening to you, and if that can be identified and dealt with the behaviour will stop

- How to control and eliminate your negative behaviour:

- **Identify the behaviour** – Ask someone who knows you well, and whom you trust, to tell you what you do, and when. The last bit, when, is very important because it helps you with step three in this process.

- **Acknowledge it** – You can't, and won't, deal with something unless you acknowledge it as a reality. It's useful to get some confirming data to help you accept what you're doing.

- **Determine the cause** – Think about when you do these things and what has occurred just prior to the behaviour.

- **Deal with the cause** – If you can get rid of the cause then you will get rid of the reaction.

- **If you can't get rid of the cause, then change the way you react to it** –Emotions are powerful things. But you *can* control them if you make an effort.

APPENDIX

The destructive myths of leadership

There's a massive amount of nonsense written about leadership. If you Google "leadership" you get almost three-quarters of a million entries. Try "leadership qualities" and you get more than 700,000. Ask for "leadership theories" and you get more than two *million*. Amazon lists over 180,000 books about leadership.

Before we go any further we need to clear the air about a number of falsehoods and fictions about leadership in those hundreds of thousands of books, or in the tens of millions of articles you can find in newspapers, magazines and journals.

Here are some of the more common myths about leadership. It's not just that they're wrong, it's that they're highly destructive.

The Making of a Leader

Myth 1: *Leaders are born, not made.*

Fact: There is an absolute *mountain* of research which shows that to be complete and utter nonsense. The reason this myth is so prevalent is due mainly to the so-called leaders who write their autobiographies – or have their biographies written for them – and who present themselves as having a talent which others don't have. We call this the invincibility syndrome, and it is generated when an individual has succeeded in a series of situations/tests where others have fallen by the wayside.

Organizations are essentially pyramidal in shape and as you advance up the hierarchy, the pyramid becomes increasingly narrow. There is only one CEO, perhaps a half dozen C-titles below that, maybe fifteen or twenty positions at the next level down, and so on. If, for illustrative purposes, someone has been promoted over his or her peers ten or fifteen times, with accompanying increased sycophancy at each promotion, they can be forgiven for thinking themselves as being, if not invincible, then at least probably infallible. Add a reward structure that pays the individual vast amounts of money and it is the rare person who can, to paraphrase the saying, keep their head while all around them are losing theirs.

Autobiographies are notoriously biased. It's highly unlikely someone is going to write negatively about themselves. They only mention the things they did that were successful, and gloss over or downplay any less successful things. While a lot of it is conscious distortion of events, there are also several psychological elements at play. One is *motivational cognition* – the natural tendency to think well of oneself and to remember the positive things and forget failures. Another is what is known as the *better than average (BTA) effect*. People see themselves as better than average on positive characteristics, and the effect is stronger for important attributes than unimportant ones.[285]

And a third element is what's referred to as *the outcome bias*. This draws us towards paying too much attention to results and too little attention to how they were achieved.[286] Research shows that looking purely at stories of success blinds us to failures that involved some of the same factors. And by not looking at failures we miss discovering the factors that caused the failure.[287] We overlook things that didn't lead to a successful outcome, but dwell on the same things when the outcome was successful.

But you can feel better about all these things and blame them on evolution. Research in the modern field of evolutionary psychology indicates that there is an evolutionary benefit from deceiving yourself.[288] The argument runs that if you can successfully deceive yourself, you will be much more effective at deceiving others and will be able to gain from that. If you think back to the days of early mankind, the ability to deceive your prey, or those things that would prey on you, is a pretty important skill. If you believe you are telling the truth you will show no sign of not doing so and you will be trusted and believed.

What makes this myth particularly wicked is that it destroys the idea that leadership can be learned, and that anyone can be a leader. It says that if you're not a born leader, then you're wasting your time getting involved in any development or training because it can't and won't make any difference. It's completely ridiculous.

Myth 2: *There are certain things that all successful leaders do – a set of traits that leaders have, and others don't.*

Fact: No. This is not a matter for debate. It is hard, scientifically proven fact. Extensive and exhaustive research into traits of effective leaders has failed to find *any* correlation between a particular set of traits and leadership success.[289] [290]

What makes this myth so destructive is that people who are deceived into believing it end up applying what they think is the 'secret recipe to leadership' – the set of so-called leadership success traits – and they stop being a leader and end up as a semi-automaton that nobody trusts. It's a guaranteed recipe for failure.

So forget searching the 700,000 Google results for "leadership qualities". Any individual, any article, or any book that tries to tell you that there is one set of behaviours which, if you exhibit them, will unfailingly result in success, is either living in dreamland or engaging in fraud. *The effectiveness of leaders' behaviour is determined by the situations in which they find themselves*, and these constantly change.[291]

Myth 3: *It's your personality that determines your performance and success (or lack of it)*

Fact: No, it isn't. Research is clear about this. [292] Your personality *doesn't* deliver results; it's what you actually *do* (your actions) that produce a consequence. The issue was dealt with in chapter 3. However, just to make one more point, if personality was the key to performance then how would you explain the performance of the following five people (who were ranked as the top five greatest leaders in the world by *Fortune* in 2017), and all of whom have very different personalities?

1. Theo Epstein, President, Baseball Operations, Chicago Cubs
2. Jack Ma, Executive Chairman, Alibaba Group
3. Pope Francis, Head of the Roman Catholic Church
4. Melinda Gates, Cochair, Bill and Melinda Gates Foundation
5. Jeff Bezos, Founder and CEO Amazon

Research shows that personality is essentially fixed very early in life.[293] But jobs change continually, so if you are limited to acting only the way your personality dictates, you're guaranteed to fail.

The Role of a Leader

Myth 4: *There are leaders and followers. You're either one or the other.*

Fact: The idea that there are leaders and followers has a variety of damaging consequences. First, it once again gets so-called leaders to believe that they, and only they, know what should be done and how to do it. And that encourages them to hold power and authority tightly, to control information, and to keep a clear barrier between themselves (the leader) and others (the followers). It's the opposite of how Ralph Nader describes leadership: "I start with the premise that the function of leadership is to produce more leaders, not more followers". As Manfred Kets de Vries puts it, "Effective business leadership is never limited to the acts of one 'heroic' individual; rather, it operates in a context of employees and of the business, industry, and larger social environment".[294]

Secondly it encourages so-called followers to abdicate responsibility – "It's not my fault". "It's not my responsibility". "I have no control over things". "I just do what I'm told". "Sorry, it's just the rules, it has nothing to do with me". This, of course, has been the defence put forward to justify all kinds of actions, from the mundane to the hugely criminal.

This myth is destructive because when people in formal positions of leadership hold power and authority tightly and believe that only they know what should be done, the consequences are never good, and can often be disastrous. A classic example in the early 1700's was a British Admiral, Sir Cloudesley Shovell. Shovell was returning with the fleet from the West Indies when a sailor approached him and said that by his calculations they were getting very close to land. But only officers were allowed to make these sorts of calculations, so the admiral had the man hanged. The next day the fleet ran aground killing virtually everyone including, rather appropriately, Cloudesley Shovell.

A more modern example is the explosion of the space shuttle Challenger. The day before the launch, Roger Boisjoly, an engineer who worked for Morton Thiokol, told the company that there were serious flaws in the O-rings the company made for the spaceship. The O-ring flaws were a cause of the explosion. But despite being right, Boisjoly was fired and never got another job in the aerospace industry. The leaders "knew" everything and "knew" non-leaders didn't.

Most people in organizations are both leaders *and* followers. Your actions have an influence on what others around you think and do, and in turn you're influenced by what they do. If you're standing on a busy street corner and you look up and keep looking up, you can be absolutely sure that a number of bystanders will also look up. Your actions will have influenced the actions of others.

Myth 5: *Managers aren't the same as leaders.*

Fact: Business school academics love splitting hairs and creating categories of things in the mistaken idea that it reflects wisdom. You can argue the semantic differences of terms such as administration, management, stewardship and leadership forever, but it won't change the fact that whatever the title of the individual, what he or she does exerts influence on others and either adds value or subtracts it, and that's leadership.

Most organizations define leaders as people who manage or super- vise others. It's rare to find a company that genuinely thinks every one of its people is, or can be a leader. As we mentioned earlier, Sberbank, Russia's biggest bank, is an outstanding exception. It has as a central pillar of its culture the statement "I am a leader". That refers to everyone from the chief executive to the cleaner in a branch office, and by encouraging its people to think that way, Sberbank and its people are able to reap the benefit of the ideas and actions of everyone.

The Impact of a Leader

Myth 6: *Leaders are charismatic and motivate their people to do things.*

Fact: Sometimes yes, and sometimes no, but generally only when the people want to do these things anyway. Harry Truman, one of America's most effective presidents, was said to have had no charisma at all. *The Independent* newspaper in Britain described Angela Merkel, the Chancellor of Germany, as "the antithesis of what we understand by charismatic".[295] *Fortune* ranked her as number 10 of the world's greatest 50 leaders in 2017.

Charisma is popularly thought of as "a spiritual power or personal quality that gives an individual influence or authority over large numbers of people". It's something "mysterious" and falls into the category of "you can't define it but you know it when you see it". One should always be deeply suspicious of that sort of explanation. The psychological fact is that you see what you want to see, not necessarily what others see, or what is generally accepted as fact.

And much of the "research and measurement" (we use the terms loosely in this case) of charisma and its results has been shown to be highly questionable.[296] Even the *Harvard Business Review*, not a publication known to shy away from showering praise on the demi-gods of management, made a nod to the fallacy about charisma in an article "Too Much Charisma Can Make Leaders Look Less Effective".[297]

Various articles have claimed that Paul Polson, CEO of Unilever, lacks charisma. But he sounds like a good leader to us. If it's results you want, during his tenure as CEO the share price of Unilever rose by 75%. These are the sorts of things he says and you can judge whether they reflect charisma or not. "I would not relate success to a title or a position"; "I basically get paid to make sure (our people) are successful"; "The moment you discover in life that it's not about yourself, that it is about investing in others, I think you're entering a steadier state to be a great leader".

The research that puts an end to the destructive myth that "charisma equals effective leadership" myth was done by Jim Collins and his team. They spent 10.5 people-years of work, analysing the results of 1,435 companies over a period from 1965 to 1995, examining 6,000 articles, and generating over 2,000 pages of interview transcripts, and their conclusion was: "*Larger-than-life, celebrity leaders ... are negatively correlated with taking a company from good to great*".[298]

Myth 7: *Leadership is one-way – top down*

Fact: No, leadership is relational; it goes in all directions: upwards (you're making a big mistake if you overlook managing upwards), laterally (how you manage the relationships with your colleagues has a major effect on your performance because virtually no jobs are conducted alone), and downwards. Rob Goffee and Gareth Jones make the point that "leadership is a relationship built actively between both parties (leaders and followers)".[299] Benjamin Disraeli, the 19th century British Prime Minister, is quoted as saying "I must follow the people. Am I not their leader?" The great former New York Yankee baseball coach, Casey Stengel said, "It's easy to get the players; it's getting them to play together that's the hard part". Within any team or organization different people take leadership at different times.

Myth 8: *Managers don't resist change, it's "employees" – meaning anyone not in a formal leadership role – that are the resistors.*

Fact: This myth is simply an excuse to exercise dominance. People are people; individuals with titles that begin with a capital C resist change as much as people who have no formal titles or managerial roles. It depends whose idea it is. Everyone likes their own ideas, and when others don't show the same level of enthusiasm they're seen as resistors. When someone with a BIG C title decides to make a change that affects someone with a small c title, or maybe an "e" title or "v" title, these people, senior as they are, can be just as resistant as others lower down the hierarchy, and are often more so because they have more to lose, in terms of power and authority.

We have an inbuilt resistance to change. Robert Kegan and Lisa Laskow Lahey call it "immunity to change".[300] They cite a medical study where heart doctors told their patients they would literally die if they didn't make changes to their lives like stopping smoking, diet, exercise, etc., but *85% still didn't make the changes.*

Resistance to change is not about logic or education or misunderstanding of facts, and it's not different for people at the top of the tree or at the bottom. Resistance to change is part of the human fabric. Get over it. You resist change as much as the next person. But you don't have to.

Myth 9: *Leadership development programmes make a big difference to organizational performance.*

Fact: In the US alone, companies spend more than $14 billion annually on leadership development.[301] In addition, there are tens of thousands of university and college courses on leadership. However, an extensive survey of research studies into the effectiveness of leaders indicated that 50% of leaders are judged to be "a disappointment, incompetent, a mis-hire, or a complete failure in their current roles".[302] Another large survey found that slightly more than a third of managers, and just a quarter of HR professionals, rated leadership in their companies as excellent or good.[303] And if you want the view from the people who are led, a survey of about 1,300 employees around the world showed that over 50% considered leaving their jobs because of their leader, and 39% actually did.[304]

One of the main reasons why leadership development programmes are a failure is that they fail to measure outputs – which behaviours have changed. The only "measures" applied tend to be the "happy sheets" at the end of the programme. The hard fact is that there is almost no connection between this type of evaluation and behaviour change.[305] Happy sheets are about evaluating entertainment. The worst feedback that a trainer can get is "that was interesting". That's code for "entertaining, but I won't be doing anything about it".

Leadership development programmes fail when they don't measure leadership development. They don't measure the behaviour change of the participants and they don't measure the effectiveness of these changes in terms of key performance indicators.

Myth 10: *In terms of leader performance, you get what you pay for.*

Fact: Senior executive and CEO pay (which gets most public coverage) does not correlate with performance. Organizational size accounts for 40% of the variation in CEO pay but performance only accounts for 5%.[306] A *New York Times* article showed that executive pay has far exceeded corporate earnings or increase in market value.[307]

A study of pay and performance in 1500 large companies from 1994 to 2013 concluded that the more CEOs are paid, the worse the firm does. The worst performing companies are the ones headed by the individuals who are at the top 10% level of pay. These companies had 10% poorer returns than their industry peers. Even more incredible, the performance in companies where the CEO was among the 5% highest paid, performance was 15% worse.[308]

If you want to spend the next few hundred years reading one of the 100,000 books about leadership each day, you will most certainly be able to add lots more common myths to this list, but we'll stop here.

Endnotes

[1]   Jeffrey Pfeffer, *Leadership BS*, Harper Collins, 2015.

[2]   Stathis, K. L., "Ocean Tomo 2015 Annual Study of Intangible Asset Market Value", www.oceantomo.com/blog/2015/03-05-ocean-tomo-2015-intangible-asset-market-value

[3]   *Workforce 2020: The Looming Talent Crisis*, Oxford Economics, 2014.

[4]   Miner, A., Glomb,T., and Hulin, C., "Experience sampling mood and its correlates at work", *Journal of Occupational and Organizational Psychology*, volume 78, 2005.

[5]   Dasborough, M. T., "Cognitive Asymmetry in Employee Emotional Reactions to Leadership Behaviours", *Leadership Quarterly*, volume 17, 2006.

[6]   Peter Nixon, *Dialogue Gap*, John Wiley & Sons Singapore Pte. Ltd., 2012.

[7]   Peter Honey, *Improve Your People Skills*, 2nd ed., CIPD, 1997.

[8]   Chan Kim and Renée Mauborgne, "Blue Ocean Leadership", *Harvard Business Review*, May 2104.

[9]   Daniel Goleman, *Social Intelligence: The New Science of Social Relationships*, Bantam Books, 2006

[10] Mark Murphy, "Why the CEO Gets Fired", *LeadershipIQ.com*, June 22, 2015.

[11] Rob Goffee and Gareth Jones, *Why Should Anyone be Led by You?,* Harvard Business School Press, 2006.

[12] "Leaders for the Long Term", *Harvard Business Review*, November 2014

[13] Daniel McGinn, "The Best Performing CEOs in the World 2017", *Harvard Business Review*, November-December 2017.

14   Michel Anteby, *Manufacturing Morals*, University of Chicago Press, 2015.

15   Warren Bennis, *On Leadership*, Basic Books 4th ed., 2009.

16   Willis, J., and Todorov, A., "First Impressions: Making Up Your Mind After a 100-ms Exposure to a Face", *Psychological Science*, volume 17, 2006.

17   Ambady, N., and Rosenthal, R., "This Slices of Expressive Behaviour as Predictors of Interpersonal Consequences: A Meta-Analysis", *Psychological Bulletin*, volume 111, 1992.

18   Ames, D. R., and Johar, G. V., "I'll Know What You're Like When I See How You Feel: How and When Affective Displays Influence Behavior-Based Impressions", *Psychological Science*, volume 20, 2009.

19   Yaniv, I., and Kleinberger, E., "Advice Taking in Decision Making: Egocentric Discounting and Reputation Formation", *Organizational Behavior and Human Decision Processes*, volume 83, 2000.

20   Suedfeld, P., Bochner, S., and Matas, C., "Petitioner's Attire and Petition Signing by Peace Demonstrators: A Field Experiment", *Journal of Applied Social Psychology*, volume 1, 1971.

21   Asch, S. E. < "Studies of independence and conformity: A minority of one against a unanimous majority", *Psychological Monographs*, volume 70, 1956.

22   Hatfield, E., et. al., *Emotional Contagion*, Cambridge University Press, 1994.

23   Barsade G., "The Ripple effect: Emotional contagion and its influence on group behaviour", *Administrative Science Quarterly*, volume 47, 2002.

24   Howard, D. J., and Gengler, C., "Emotional Contagion Effects on Product Attitudes", *Journal of Consumer Research*, volume 28, 2001.

25   Dasborough, M. T., et. al., "What goes around comes around: How meso-level emotional contagion can ultimately determine organizational attitudes toward leaders", *The Leadership Quarterly*, volume 20, 2009.

26   Cuddy, A. J. C., Kohut, M., and Neffinger, J., "Connect, Then lead: To Exert Influence You Must Balance Competence with Warmth", *Harvard Business Review*, July-August, 2013.

27   Todorov, A., Pakrashi, M., and Oosterhof, N., N., "Evaluating Faces on Trustworthiness After Minimal Time Exposure" *Social Cognition*, volume 27, 2009.

28   Grandey, A. A., et. al., "Is Service With a Smile Enough? Authenticity of Positive Displays During Service Encounters", *Organizational Behaviour and Human Decision Processes*, Volume 96, 2005.

29 Chuck Leddy, "The Power of Thanks", *Harvard Gazette*, March 2013.

30 Gutman, R., "The Untapped Power of Smiling", *Forbes*, March 22, 2011.

31 Abel. E. L., Kruger, M.L., "Smile Intensity in Photographs Predicts Longevity", *Psychological Science*, volume 21, 2010.

32 Dimburg, U., and Söderkvist, S., "The Voluntary Facial Action Technique: A Method to Test the Facial Feedback Hypothesis", *Journal of Nonverbal Behaviour*, volume 35, 2011.

33 Halevy, N., et. al., "Status Conferral in Intergroup Social Dilemmas: Behavioural Antecedents and Consequences of Prestige and Dominance", *Journal of Personality and Social Psychology*, volume 102, 2012.

34 Ferris, G. R., et. al., "Development and Validation of the Political Skill Inventory", *Journal of Management,* volume 31, 2005.

35 Adam Grant, *Give and Take: A revolutionary approach to success*, Viking, 2013.

36 Robin Stuart-Kotze, *Performance: The Secrets of Successful Behaviour*, FT Prentice-Hall (Pearson), 2006.

37 Obituary, Major John Sim, MC, *The Times*, January 23, 2017.

38 Stiverson, L., "Give people freedom and they will amaze you: Prasad Shetty", *Business Radio Powered by The Wharton School, 2016.*

39 Wood, Z., "The John Lewis model and what others could learn from it", *The Guardian*, January 16, 2012.

40 Detert, J. R., and Burns, E. R., "Can Your Employees Really Speak Freely?", *Harvard Business Review*, January-February 2016.

41 Wasko, M. M, and Faraj, J, "It is what one does: Why people participate and help others in electronic communities of practice", *The Journal of Strategic Information Systems*, volume 9, 2000.

42 Detert, J. R., and Burris, E. R., "Leadership Behaviour and Employee Voice: Is the Door Really Open?", *Academy of Management Journal*, volume 50, 2007.

43 Lloyd, K. J., et. al., "is My Boss Really Listening to Me? The Impact of Perceived Supervisor Listening on Emotional Exhaustion, Turnover Intention, and organizational Citizenship Behaviour", *Journal of Business Ethics*, volume 130, 2015.

44 Nadler, A., Ellis, S., and Bar, I., "To Seek or Not to Seek: The relationship Between Help Seeking and Job Performance Evaluations as Moderated by

Task-Relevant Expertise", *Journal of Applied Social Psychology*, volume 33, 2003.

45 Adam Grant, *Give and Take*, Viking, 2013.

46 Muraven, M, Gagné, M, and Rosman, H., "helpful Self-Control: Autonomy, Support, Vitality and Depletion", *Journal of Experimental and Social Psychology*, volume 44, 2008.

47 Charles Duhigg, *The Power of Habit: Why we do what we do and how to change*, Random House, 2012.

48 Flynn, F. J., "How Much Should I Give and How Often? The Effects of Generosity and Frequency of Favor Exchange on Social Status and Productivity", *Academy of Management Journal*, volume 46, 2003.

49 Bohn, V. K., and Flynn, F.J., "Why didn't you just ask? Underestimating the discomfort of help-seeking", *Journal of Experimental Social Psychology*, volume 46, 2010.

50 Flynn, F.J. and Lake, K. B., "If you need help, just ask: Underestimating compliance with direct requests for help", *Journal of Personality and Social Psychology*, volume 95, 2008.

51 Langer, E, and Abelson R. P., "The semantics of asking for a favour: How to succeed in getting help without actually dying ", *Journal of Personality and Social Psychology*, volume 24, 1972.

52 Liljenquist, K. A., and Galinsky, A., "Turn Your Adversary into Your Advocate", *Negotiation*, 2007.

53 Robert Cialdini, *Influence: The psychology of persuasion*, Collins 2001.

54 Regan, D. T., "Effects of a Favour and Liking on Compliance", *Journal of Experimental Social Psychology*, volume 7, 1971.

55 Gergen, K. J., et. al., "Obligation, Donor Resources, and Reactions to Aid in Three Cultures", *Journal of Personality and Social Psychology*, volume 31, 1975.

56 Know, R. E., and Inkster, A. J., "Post Decisional Dissonance Reduction", *Journal of Personality and Social Psychology*, volume 8, 1968.

57 Aarts, H, and Dijksterhuis, A., "The silence of the library: Environment, situational norm, and social behaviour", *Journal of Personality and Social Psychology*, volume 84 2003,

[58] Bartholow, B. D., et. al., "Interactive effects of life experience and situational cues on aggression: The weapons priming effect on hunters and non-hunters", *Journal of Experimental Social Psychology*, volume 41, 2005.

[59] Gino, F., Norton, M. I., and Ariely, D., "The counterfeit Self: The Deceptive Costs of Faking It", *Psychological Science*, volume 21, 2010

[60] Berger, J., Meredith, M., and Wheeler, S. C., "Contextual priming: Where people vote affects how they vote, *Proceedings of the National Academy of Sciences*, July 2008.

[61] Williams, L. E., and Bargh, J. A., "Experiencing Physical Warmth Promotes Interpersonal Warmth", *Science*, volume 322, 2008.

[62] Critcher, C. R., and Gilovich, T., "Incidental environmental anchors", *Journal of Behavioral Decision Making*, volume 21, 2008.

[63] Vance Packard, *The Status Seekers*, David McKay, 1959.

[64] Drachman, D., deCarufel, A., and Insko, A. C., "The extra credit effect in interpersonal attraction", *Journal of Experimental Social Psychology*, volume 14, 1978.

[65] Fogg, B. J., and Nass, C., "Silicon sycophants: The effects of computers that flatter", *International Journal of Human-Computer Studies*, volume 46, 1997.

[66] Grant, A. M., Berg, J. M., and Cable, D. M., "Job Titles as identity Badges: How Self-Reflective Titles Can Reduce Emotional Exhaustion", *Academy of Management Journal*, volume 57, 2014.

[67] Susan Adams, "New Survey: Majority of Employees Dissatisfied", *Forbes*, May 2012.

[68] Mark Crowley, "Gallup's Workplace Jedi on How to Fix Our Employee Engagement Problem", *www.fastcompany.com*, June 2013.

[69] Mischel, W., and Liebert, R. M., "Effects of Discrepancies between Observed and Imposed Reward Criteria on Their Acquisition and Transmission", *Journal of Personality and Social Psychology*, volume 3, 1966.

[70] Mischel, W., and Liebert, R. M., "The Role of Power in the Adoption of Self-Reward Patterns", *Child Development*, volume 38, 1967.

[71] Geoff Colvin, "Mary Barra's (unexpected) Opportunity), *Fortune*, October 6, 2014

[72] Ibid.

[73] Greene, F. J., and Hopp, C., "Are Formal Planners More Likely to Achieve Venture Viability? A Counterfactual Model and Analysis", *Strategic Entrepreneurship Journal*, volume 11, 2017.

[74] Lazear,E. P., Shaw, K.L., and Stanton, C. T., "The Value of Bosses", *Journal of Labour Economics*, June, 2014,

[75] Michael Argyle, et. al., "The Communication of Inferior and Superior Attitudes by Verbal and Nonverbal Signals", *British Journal of Clinical Psychology*, volume 9, 1970.

[76] Aguinas, H., Simonsen, M. M., and Pierce, C. A., "Effects of Nonverbal Behaviour on Perceptions of Power Bases", *Journal of Social Psychology*, volume 138, 1998.

[77] Burgoon, J. K., Birk, T. and Pfau, M., "Nonverbal Behaviours, Persuasion, and Credibility", *Human Communication Research*, volume 17, 1990.

[78] Keating, K., et al. "Developmental Readiness for Leadership: The Differential Effects of Leadership Courses on Creating 'Ready, Willing, and Able' Leaders", *Journal of Leadership Education*, October 2014

[79] Glaser, R., et al., "Psychological Stress-induced Modulation of Interleukin 2 Receptor Gene Expression and Interleukin 2 Production in Peripheral Blood Leukocytes", *Archives of General Psychiatry*, volume 47, 1990.

[80] Sotnikov, S. B., et. al., "Bidirectional rescue of extreme genetic predispositions to anxiety: impact of CRH receptor 1 as epigenetic plasticity gene in the amygdala", *Translational Psychiatry*, volume 4, 2014.

[81] Robinson, G. E., Fernald, R.D., and Clayton D. F., "Genes and Social Behavior", *Science*, volume 322, 2008.

[82] Lopez-Maury, L., Marguerat, S., and Bähler, J., "Tuning gene expression to changing environments: from rapid responses to evolutionary adaptation", *Nature Review Genetics*, volume 9, 2008.

[83] Sotnikov 2014.

[84] "Headless", *The Economist*, August 3, 2006.

[85] "O wad some power the giftie gie us / To see oursels as ithers see us. / It wad frae mony a blunder free us"

[86] Macnamara, B. N., Hambrick, D. Z., and Oswald, F.L., "Deliberate Practice and Performance in Music, Games, Sports, Education, and Professions: A Meta-Analysis", *Psychological Science*, volume 25, 2014.

87   Mankins, M.C., and Steels, R., "Turning Great Strategy into Great Performance", *Harvard Business Review*, July-August 2005.

88   Walter Mischel, *Personality and Assessment*, Lawrence Earlbaum, 1968.

89   Richard Nisbett, Cited in Funder, et. al, "Personality psychology in the workplace. Decade of behaviour", *American Psychological Association*, 2001.

90   Elizabeth Bernstein, "Why Introverts Make Great Entrepreneurs", Wall Street Journal, August 24, 2015

91   Lloyd Price, "You've got personality", 1959.

92   Dean Burnett, *The Idiot Brain*, Guardian Books, 2016.

93   Mischel, 1968

94   Bass, B. M., *Bass & Stogdill's handbook of leadership: Theory, research, and managerial applications* (3rd ed.) Free Press, 1990.

95   Stephen Covey, *The Seven Habits of Highly Effective People*, Rosetta Books, 1988.

96   Druckman, D., and Bjork, R. A., (eds.), *In the Mind's Eye: Enhancing Human Performance*, National Academy press, 1991.

97   Forer, B. R., "The fallacy of personal validation: A classroom demonstration of gullibility", *Journal of Abnormal and Social Psychology*, volume 44, 1949.

98   Peterson, C., Seligman, M. E., and Valliant, G. E., "Pessimistic Explanatory Style Is a Risk Factor for Physical Illness: A Thirty-Five-Year Longitudinal Study", *Journal of Personality and Social Psychology*, volume 55. 1998.

99   Scheier, M. E., Weintraub, J. K., and Carver, C. S., "Coping with Stress: Divergent Strategies of Optimists and Pessimists", *Journal of Personality and Social Psychology*, volume 51, 1986.

100   Taylor, S. E., and Armor, D. A., "Positive Illusions and Coping with Adversity", *Journal of Personality*, volume 64, 1996.

101   Porath, C., et. al., "Thriving at work: Toward its measurement, construct validation and theoretical refinement", *Journal of Organizational Behaviour*, volume 33, 2012.

102   Spreitzer, G., and Porath, C., "Creating Sustainable Performance", *Harvard Business Review*, January-February 2012.

103   Ibid.

[104] Huang, J. L., et. al., "Personality and adaptive performance at work: A meta-analytic investigation", *Journal of Applied Psychology*, volume 99, January 2014

[105] Malhotra, S., Reus, T. H., and Zhu, PC., "The Acquisitive Nature of Extraverted CEOs", *Administrative Science Quarterly,* published online May 24, 2017.

[106] Caspi, A, et. al., "Children's behavioural styles at age three are linked to their adult personality traits at age 26", *Journal of Personality*, volume 71, 2003.

[107] Taki, Y., et. al., "A longitudinal study of the relationship between personality traits and the annual rate of volume change in regional gray matter in healthy adults", *Human Brain Mapping*, volume 34, 2013.

[108] McCrae, R. R., et. al., "Nature over nurture: Temperament, personality, and life span development", *Journal of Personality and Social Psychology,* volume 78, 2000.

[109] J. M. Rohrer, B. Egloff, and S. C. Schmukle, "Examining the effects of birth order on personality", *Proceedings of the National Academy of Sciences*, volume 112, 2015.

[110] Edgar H. Schein, *Career Anchors: Discovering Your Real Values*, Pfeiffer & Co, 1990.

[111] Stuart-Kotze, R., *Job Type as an Intervening Variable in the Prediction of Managerial Success, Using Measures of Cognitive Abilities, Personality, and Self-Perceived Leadership Style*, University of Warwick, 1981.

[112] Dean Burnett, 2016.

[113] Murray, J. B., "Review of research on the Myers-Briggs type Indicator", *Perceptual and Motor Skills*, volume 70, 1990.

[114] Dean Burnett, 2016.

[115] Trachtenberg, J. A., and Beckerman, J., "Barnes and noble Say CEO Boire Not a Good Fit, and Will Step Down", *Wall Street Journal*, August 16, 2016.

[116] CEO Succession Report 2011, Booz Allen Hamilton

[117] "Leadership Transitions", McKinsey Leadership Development, *mld.mckinsey.com*

[118] Peter Drucker, *The Effective Executive: The Definitive Guide to Getting the Right Things Done*, Harperbusiness Essentials, 2006

[119] Alejandro Serralde, "Effect of leaders' ability to adjust behaviour to match changing situational demands", Private correspondence, 2016.

[120] Daniel Kahneman, *Thinking, Fast and Slow*, Farrar, Straus and Giroux, 2011

[121] Salovey, P., and Mayer, J. D., "Emotional Intelligence", *Imagination, Cognition and Personality*, volume 9, 1990.

[122] Gardner, L., and Stough, C., "Examining the relationship between leaders and emotional intelligence in senior level managers", *Leadership and Organization Development Journal*, volume 23, 2002.

[123] Rosete, D., and Ciarrochi, J., "Emotional intelligence and its relationship to workplace performance outcomes of leadership effectiveness", *Leadership and Organization Development Journal,* volume 26, 2005.

[124] Marmot, M. G., et. al., "Contribution of Job Control and Other Risk Factors to Social Variations in Coronary Heart Disease Incidence", *The Lancet,* volume 350, 1997.

[125] Cohen, S., Tyrrell, D. A. J., and Smith, A. P.," Psychological Stress and Susceptibility to the Common Cold", *New England Journal of Medicine*, volume 325, 1991.

[126] McDonald, N. W., Heimstra, A. L., and Damkot, D. K., "Social Modification of Antagonistic Behaviour in Fish", *Animal Behaviour*, volume16, 1968.

[127] Ian Robertson, *The Winner Effect*, Bloomsbury, 2012.

[128] Booth, A., et. el., "Testosterone, and winning and losing in human competition", *Hormones and Behaviour*, volume 23, 1989.

[129] Paul C. Bernhardt, P. C., et. al., "Testosterone changes during vicarious experiences of winning and losing among fans at sporting events", *Physiology and Behaviour*, volume 65, 1998.

[130] Galinsky, A. D. et. al., "Power and Perspectives Not Taken", *Psychological Science*, volume 17, 2006.

[131] Gruenfeld, D., et. al., "Power and the Objectification of Social Targets", *Journal of Personality and Social Psychology*, volume 95, 2008.

[132] Hackett, R., "The 1% are 55% less helpful", *Fortune*, September 1, 2016.

[133] Hildreth, J. A. D., and Anderson, C. "Failure at the Top: How Power Undermines Collaborative Performance", *Journal of personality and Social Psychology*, volume 110, 2016.

134 Mizuyama, R., et. al., Noradrenaline Improves Behavioral Contrast Sensitivity via the B-Adrenergic Receptor", PLoS ONE, volume 11, 2016.

135 Fast, N. J., and Chen, S., "When the Boss Feels Inadequate ", *Psychological Science*, volume 20, 2009.

136 *Foulk, T, and Lanaj, K, "Feeling Powerful at Work Makes Us Feel Worse When We get Home", Harvard Business Review,* June 13, 2017.

137 Jeffrey Pfeffer, *What Were They Thinking? Unconventional wisdom about management*, Harvard Business School Press, 2007.

138 Herzberg, F., "One More Time: How Do You Motivate Employees?" , *Harvard Business Review*, January–February 1968.

139 "Employee Engagement in US Stagnant is 2015", *Gallup*, January 2016.

140 Dewhurst, M., Guthridge, M., and Mohr, E., "Motivating People: Getting Beyond the Money", *McKinsey Quarterly*, November 2009.

141 Wallstreetoasis.com

142 James Surowiecki, "The Cult of Overwork", *The New Yorker*, January 27, 2014.

143 Gagné, M., and Deci, E. L., "Self-Determination Theory and Work Motivation", *Journal of Behavioural Science*, volume 26, 2005

144 Ophir, E., Nass, C., and Wagner, A. D., "Cognitive control in media multitaskers", *Proceedings of the National Academy of Sciences*, September 2009.

145 Michael Corkery, "Wells Fargo Fined $185 Million for Fraudulently Opening Accounts", *DealB%k*, September 2016.

146 In Reeve, S.G., et. al, *Motivation and Emotion*, 1986.

147 Chikungwa, T., and Shingirayi, F. C., ""An Evaluation of Recognition on Performance as a Motivator: A Case of Eastern Cape Higher Education Institution", *Mediterranean Journal of Social Sciences*, volume 4, 2013.

148 Baskar, D., and Rajkumar, K. R., "A Study on the Impact of Rewards and Recognition on Employee Motivation", *International Journal of Science and Research*, volume 4, 2015.

149 Ashby, F. G., Isen, A. M., and Turken, A. U., "A Neuropsychological Theory of Positive Affect and Its Influence on Cognition", *Psychological Bulletin*, volume 106, 1999.

150 Chuck Leddy, "The Power of Thanks", *Harvard Gazette*, March 2013

151 Izuma, K., Saito, DN., and Sadato, N., "Processing of social and monetary rewards in the human striatum", *Neuron*, volume 58, 2208.

152 Neckerman, S., and Yang, X., "Understanding the (unexpected) consequences of Unexpected recognition", *Journal; of Economic Behaviour and Organization,* volume 135, 2017.

153 Leslie Patton, "The Latest Shortage: Fast-Food Workers, *Bloomberg Business Week*, January 16, 2017.

154 Roberta Holland, "Money and Quotas Motivate the Sales Force Best", *Working Knowledge*, Harvard Business School, July 6, 2015.

155 Buell, R. W., Kim, T., and Tsay, C-J., "Creating Reciprocal Value Through Operational Transparency", *Social science Research Network*, published online May 2016.

156 Ibid

157 Eisenberger, N. I., "Social Pain and the Brain: Controversies, Questions, and Where to Go from Here", *Annual Review of Psychology*, volume 66, 2015.

158 Smith, G. D., et. al., "Socioeconomic differentials in mortality: Evidence from Glasgow graveyards", *British Medical Journal*, volume 305, 1992.

159 Redelmeir, D. A., and Singh, S. M., "Survival in Academy Award-winning actors and actresses", *Annals of Internal Medicine*, volume 134, 2006.

160 Rablen, M. D., and Oswald, A. J., "Mortality and Immortality; The Nobel Prize as an experiment into the effect of status upon longevity", *Journal of Health Economics*, volume 27, 2008.

161 Kang, M. J., et. al., "The Wick in the Candle of Learning: Epistemic Curiosity Activates Reward Circuitry and Enhances Memory", *Psychological Science*, volume 20, August 2009.

162 Murayama, K., et. al., "Neural basis of the undermining effect of monetary reward on intrinsic motivation", *Proceedings of the National Academy of Sciences*, volume 107, 2010.

163 Maruthappu, M., et. al., "Economic downturns, universal health coverage, and cancer mortality in high-income and middle-income countries, 1990-2010: A longitudinal analysis", *The Lancet*, volume 388, 2016.

164 Ryan, R. M. and Deci, E. L., "Self-determination theory and the facilitation of intrinsic motivation, social development, and well-being", *American Psychologist*, volume 55, 2000.

165 Ibid.

166 Tummers, L, et. al., "The Effects of Leadership and Job Autonomy on Vitality", *Review of Public Personnel Administration*, published online, October 2016.

167 Lepper. M. R., Greene, D., and Nisbett, R. E., "Undermining children's intrinsic interest with extrinsic reward: A test of the 'over-justification' hypothesis", *Journal of Personality and Social Psychology*, volume 28, 1973.

168 McClelland, D. C., *The Achieving Society*, Van Nostrand, 1961.

169 Ibid.

170 David C. McClelland and David H. Burnham, "Power is the Great Motivator", *Harvard Business Review*, January 2003.

171 Ibid.

172 Ibid.

173 John P. Kotter and James L. Heskett, *Corporate Culture and Performance*, The Free Press, 1992

174 Thomas J. Peters and Robert H. Waterman Jr., *In Search of Excellence; Lessons from America's best run companies*, Harper Collins, 1982.

175 Gartenberg, C., Prat, A., and Serafeim, G., "Corporate Purpose and Financial Performance", *HBS Working Paper #17-023*, September 2016.

176 *Fortune*, August 1, 2016.

177 Ibid.

178 Richard Barrett, *Building a Values-driven Organization: A Whole-system Approach to Cultural Transformation*, Butterworth-Heinemann, 2006.

179 Boyce, A. S., et. al,, "Which comes first, organizational culture or performance: A longitudinal study of causal priority with automobile dealerships", *Journal of Organizational Behaviour*, volume 36, 2015.

180 Rogers, P, Meehan, P, and Tanner, S., "Building a Winning Culture", *Bain and Company*, 2006

181 Ibid.

182 Geoff Colvin, "Personal Bests", *Fortune*, March 2015.

183 Porath, C. L., et.al.," Civility as an Enabler of Social Capital: How it Spreads – and What Limits Its Potential", *working paper, Georgetown University*, Washington, DC, 2016.

184 Bear, A., and Rand, D. G., "Intuition, Deliberation, and the Evolution of Cooperation", *Proceedings of the National Academy of Sciences*, volume 113, 2016.

185 Kathleen Redmond, *Building a Character Culture*, 2013, *Communicating a Character Culture*, 2015, *Character Coaching*, 2017, IC Publishing,

186 Fred Kiel, *Return on Character: The Real Reason Leaders and Their Companies Win*, HBR Press, 2015.

187 "Defend Your Research: MBAs are more self-serving than other CEOs" *Harvard Business Review*, December 2016.

188 Baron, J. N., and Hannan, M. T., "Organizational Blueprints for Success in High-Tech Startups: Lessons from the Stanford Project on Emerging Companies", *California Management Review*, volume 44, 2002.

189 Jim Collins, "Aligning Action and Values", *Leader to Leader*, Summer, 1996.

190 *The Wall Street Journal*, September 21, 2015.

191 Wilkes, W, "Volkswagen's Emissions Bill Could Surpass $25 Billion", *Wall Street Journal*, February 1, 2017.

192 Armstrong, R., "The Volkswagen scandal shows that corporate culture matters", *The Financial Times,* January 14, 2017.

193 Barsade, S., and O'Neill, O. A., "Manage Your Emotional Culture", *Harvard Business Review*, January-February 2016.

194 Gregory. A., and Wright, J., "Defining Organizational Character", *The Melbourne Mandate*, July 2012.

195 Kotter and Heskett, 1992.

196 Stewart, G. L., "A Meta-Analytic Review of Relationships Between Team Design Features and Team Performance", *Journal of Management*, volume 32, 2006.

197 Dirks, K. T., "Trust in Leadership and Team Performance: Evidence From NCAA Basketball", *Journal of Applied Psychology*, volume 85, 2000.

198 Geoffrey Colvin, *Humans are Underrated*, Penguin Random House, 2015.

199 Mesmer-Magnus, J. R., and DeChurch, L. A., "Information sharing and team performance: A meta-analysis", *Journal of Applied Psychology*, volume 94, 2009.

200 Edmondson, A., "Psychological Safety and Learning Behavior in Work Teams", *Administrative Science Quarterly*, volume 44, 1999.

201 Ibid.

202 Ibid..

203 Zautra, E. K., et. al., "Can We Learn to Treat One Another Better? A Test of a Social Intelligence Curriculum", *PloS ONE, June* 2015.

204 Amy Zipkin, "The Wisdom of Thoughfulness", New York Times, May 31, 2000.

205 http://communicationtheory.org/the-johari-window-model

206 Woolley, A. W., et. al., "Evidence for a Collective Intelligence Factor in the Performance of Human Groups", *Science*, volume 330, 2010

207 N. J. Cooke, et. al., "Interactive team cognition", *Cognitive Science*, volume 37, 2013.

208 Richard Hackman, *Leading Teams, Setting the Stage for Great Performances*, Harvard Business School Press, 2002.

209 Richard Hackman, *Groups that work (and those that don't)*, Jossey-Bass,1990.

210 Cross, R., Rebele, R., and Grant, A., "Collaborative Overload", *Harvard Business Review*, January-February 2016.

211 Dyer, J. L., "Team research and team training: A state of the art review", In F. A. Muckler (Ed.), *Human factors review*, 1984.

212 Katzenbach J. R., and Smith, D. K., *The Wisdom of Teams*, Harvard Business School Press, 1993

213 Richard Hackman, 1990.

214 Kets de Vries, M., The Hedgehog Effect: Building High Performance Teams, *The European Business Review*, September 2012.

215 Bradley, B. H., et. al., "Ready to rumble: How team personality composition and task conflict interact to improve performance", *Journal of Applied Psychology*, volume 98, 2013.

216 David Kirk, "World Class Teams", *McKinsey Quarterly*. December 1992.

217 De Dreu, C. K. W., and Weingart, L. R., "Task Versus Relationship Conflict, Team Performance, and Team Member Satisfaction: A Meta-Analysis", *Journal of Applied Psychology*, volume 88, 2003.

218 Kets de Vries, M., "High Performance Teams: Lessons from the Pygmies", *INSEAD Working Paper*, 1999.

219 Internal Sberbank corporate document.

220 Evan Wittenberg, "Is your team too big? Too small? What's the right number?", *Knowledge@Wharton*, 2006.

221 Leslie Perlow, "Manage Your Team's Collective Time", *Harvard Business Review*, June 2014.

222 Stuart-Kotze, R., *Performance: The Secrets of Successful Behaviour*, Pearson, 2006.

223 Katzenbach and Smith, 1993.

224 Vogel, A. L., et.al., "Pioneering the transdisciplinary team science approach: Lessons learned from National Cancer Institute grantees", *Journal of Translational Medicine & Epidemiology*, volume 2, 2014.

225 Carson, J. B., Tesluk, P. E., and Marrone, J. A., "Shared Leadership in Teams: An Investigation of Antecedent Conditions and Performance", *Academy of Management Journal*, volume 50, 2007.

226 Qiu, T., et. al., "Performance of Cross-Functional Development Teams; A Multi-Level Mediated Model", *Journal of Product Innovation Management*, volume 26, 2009.

227 deWit, F. R., Greer, L. L., and K.A. Jehn, K. A., "The paradox of intergroup conflict: A metaanalysis", *Journal of Applied Psychology*, volume 97, 2012.

228 M. A. Marks, M.A., Mathieu, J.E., and Zaccaro, S. J., "A temporally based framework and taxonomy of team processes", *Academy of Management Review*, volume 26, 2001.

229 Katzenbach and Smith, 1993.

230 Edmondson, A. C., and Nembhard, I., "Product development and learning in project teams: The challenges are the benefits", *Journal of Production Innovation Management*, volume 26, 2009.

231 Edmondson, A. C., "Psychological safety and learning behavior in work teams", *Administrative Science Quarterly*, volume 44, 1999.

232 Pritchard, R. D., et. al., "The productivity measurement and enhancement system: A meta-analysis", *Journal of Applied Psychology*, volume 93, 2008.

233 Losada, M., and Heaphy, E., "The Role of Positivity and Connectivity in the Performance of Business Teams: A Nonlinear Dynamics Model", *American Behavioural Scientist*, volume 47, 2004.

234 Harris, A., "Distributed Leadership: According to the Evidence", *Journal of Educational Administration*, volume 46, 2008.

[235] Katzenbach and Smith, 1993.

[236] Edmund Lau, "When and Where is Teamwork Important?", *Forbes*, January 23, 2013,

[237] Goh, J., Pfeffer, G., and Zenios, S. A., "The Relationship Between Workplace Stressors and Mortality and Health Costs in the United States", *Management Science*, Published on line in Articles in Advance, March 13, 2015.

[238] Blanding, M., "Workplace Stress Responsible for up to $190B in Annual US Health Care Costs", *Forbes*, January 26, 2015.

[239] Work related Stress, Anxiety and Depression Statistics in Great Britain 2016, *Health and Safety Executive, V1*, November 2016.

[240] Miner, A., Glomb, T., and Hulin, C., "Experience sampling mood and its correlates at work", *Journal of Occupational and Organizational Psychology*, volume 78, 2005.

[241] Dasborough, M. T., "Cognitive Asymmetry in Employee Emotional Reactions to Leadership Behaviours", *Leadership Quarterly*, volume 17, 2006.

[242] Kivimaki, M., et. el., "Justice at work and reduced risk of coronary heart disease among employees: the Whitehall II Study", *Archives of Internal Medicine*, volume 165, 2005.

[243] Mitchell, M. S., and Ambrose, M. L., "Abusive supervision and workplace deviance and the moderating effects of negative reciprocity beliefs", *Journal of Applied Psychology*, volume 92, 2007.

[244] Stanley, M. L., et. al., "Defining Nodes in Complex Brain Networks", *Frontiers in Computational Neuroscience*, Published online, November 22, 2013.

[245] Foulk, T., Erez, A., and Woolum, A., "Catching Rudeness is Like Catching a Cold: The Contagion Effects of Low-Intensity Negative Behaviours", *Journal of Applied Psychology*, volume 101, 2016.

[246] Porath, C. L., and Erez, A., "How Rudeness takes its toll", *The Psychologist*, volume 24, 2011.

[247] Rosenstein, A. H., and O'Daniel, M., "A Survey of the Impact of Disruptive Behaviours and Communication Defects on Patient Safety", *Joint Commission Journal on Quality and Patient Safety*, Volume 34, 2008.

[248] Riskin, A., et. al., "The Impact of Rudeness on Medical Team Performance: A Randomized Trial", *Pediatrics*, volume 136, 2015.

[249] Christine Porath, "No Time to be Nice at Work", *New York Times*, June 19, 2015

[250] Porath, C. L., Gerbasi, A. and Schorch, S.L., "The Effects of Civility on Advice, Leadership and Performance", *Journal of Applied Psychology*, volume 100, number 5, 2015.

[251] Porath, C. L., "Managing Yourself: An Antidote to Incivility", *Harvard Business Review*, April 2016.

[252] Porath, C., "No Time to be Nice at Work", *New York Times*, June 19, 2015.

[253] Porath, C. L. and Erez, A., "Does Rudeness Really Matter? The Effects of Rudeness on Task Performance and Helpfulness", *Academy of Management Journal,* volume 50, 2007.

[254] Porath, C. L., and Erez, A., "Overlooked but not untouched: How rudeness reduces onlooker's performance on routine and creative tasks", *Organizational Behaviour and Human Decision Processes*, volume 109, May 2009.

[255] Dickerson, S. S., "Emotional and Physiological Responses to Social-Evaluative Threat", *Social and Personality Psychology Compass*, volume 2, 2008.

[256] Dickerson, S. S., and Kemeny, M. E., "Acute Stresses and Cortisol Responses: a Theoretical Integration and Synthesis of Laboratory Research", *Psychological Bulletin,* volume 130, 2004.

[257] Selye, H., "A Syndrome Produced by Diverse Nocuous Agents", *Nature*, volume 138, 1936.

[258] Sapolsky, R. M., "Why Stress is Bad for Your Brain", *Science*, volume 273, 1996.

[259] Walter Mischel, "The Marshmallow Test", Bantam Press, 2014.

[260] Robert Sutton, *The No-Asshole Rule: Building a Civilised Workplace and Surviving One That Isn't*, Sphere, 2007.

[261] www.bullyinworkplace.com

[262] ibid

[263] C. M. Pearson, C. M., and Porath, C. L., "On the Nature, Consequences, and Remedies of Workplace Incivility: No Time for 'Nice'? Think Again", *The Academy of Management Executive*, Volume 19, 2005.

[264] Pearson, C. M., and Porath, C. L., "On incivility, its impact and directions for future research", in *The Dark Side of Organizational Behaviour*, Griffin and O'Leary-Kelly, Wiley, 2004

265 Mawritz, M. B., et.al., "Trickle down model of abusive supervision", *Personnel Psychology*, volume 65, 2012

266 Adam Grant, *Originals: How Non-conformists change the world*, W H Allen, 2016.

267 Bushman, B. J., "Does venting anger feed or extinguish the flame? Catharsis, Rumination, Distraction, Anger, and Aggressive Responding", *Personality and Social Psychology Bulletin*, volume 28, 2002.

268 Vitalsmarts Research, www.vitalsmarts.com, March 2010

269 Glenn Marron, "Conflict Avoidance", www.glennmarron.com, May 26. 2014

270 Jordan, P. J., and Troth, A. C., "Emotional Intelligence and Conflict Resolution: Implications for Human Resource Development", *Advances in Developing Human Resources*, volume 4, 2002.

271 Nowack, K. M., "Coping style, cognitive hardiness, and health status", *Journal of Behavioral Medicine*, volume 12, 1989.

272 Hyde, M., et. al., "Workplace conflict resolution and the health of employees in the Swedish and Finnish units of an industrial company", *Social Science & Medicine*, volume 63, 2006.

273 Chang, E. M., et.al., "The Relationships Among Workplace Stressors, Coping Methods, Demographic Characteristics, and Health in Australian Nurses", *Journal of Professional Nursing*, volume 22, 2006.

274 Cavanagh, S. J., "The conflict management style of staff nurses and nurse managers", *Journal of Advanced Nursing*, volume 16, 1991.

275 Sidle, S. D., "The Danger of Do Nothing Leaders", *Academy of Management Perspectives*, volume 21, 2007.

276 Anderson, C. J., "The psychology of doing nothing: Forms of decision avoidance result from reason and emotion", *Psychological Bulletin*, volume 129, 2003.

277 Zenger, J., and Folkman, J., "How Damaging is a Bad Boss, Exactly?", *Harvard Business Review*, July 16, 2012

278 Schwartz, T., "Why Appreciation Matters So Much", *Harvard Business Review*, January 23, 2012.

279 Bear, A., and Rand, D. G., "Intuition, deliberation and the evolution of cooperation", *Proceedings of the National Academy of Sciences*, November 2015.

280 Christine Porath, *Mastering Civility: A manifesto for the workplace*, Grand Central Publishing, New York, 2016.

281 Ryan, K., and Oestrich, D., *Driving Fear out of the Workplace*, Jossey-Bass, 1991

282 Matta, F. K., et. al., "In Consistently Unfair Better than Sporadically Fair? An Investigation of Justice Variability and Stress", *Academy of Management Journal*, volume 60, 2017.

283 Porath, C. L., "Managing Yourself: An Antidote to Incivility", *Harvard Business Review*, April 2016.

284 Viktor Frankl, *Man's Search for Meaning*, Beacon Press, 2006.

285 Brown, J. D., "Understanding the Better Than Average Effect: Motives (Still) Matter", *Personality and Social Psychology Bulletin*, volume 38, 2012.

286 Gino, F., "What we Miss When We Judge a Decision by the Outcome", *Harvard Business Review*, September 2016.

287 Denrell, J., "Vicarious Learning, Undersampling of Failure, and the Myths of Management", *Organization Science*, volume 14, 2003.

288 von Heppel, W., and Trivers, R., "The Evolution and Psychology of Self-Deception", *Behavioural and Brain Sciences*, volume 34, 2011.

289 Bass, B. M., *Bass & Stogdill's handbook of leadership: Theory, research, and managerial applications* (3rd ed.), Free Press, 1990.

290 Stogdill, R. M., "Personal factors associated with leadership: A survey of the literature", *Journal of Psychology, 25*, 1948; Bass & Stogdill', ibid.

291 Ibid.

292 Walter Mischel, *Personality and Assessment*, (Lawrence Erlbaum, 1968).

293 Caspi, A, et. al., "Children's behavioural styles at age three are linked to their adult personality traits at age 26", *Journal of Personality*, vol. 71, 2003.

294 Kets de Vries, M., *The Leadership Mystique*, 2nd ed., Pearson, 2006.

295 Katherine Butler, "Angela Merkel and the myth of charismatic leadership", *The Independent*, September 12, 2013

296 van Kippenberg, D., and Sirkin, S., "A Critical Assessment of Charismatic-Transformational Leadership Research: Back to the Drawing Board?", *Academy of Management Annals*, Volume 7, 2013.

297 Vergauwe, J., et. al., "Too Much Charisma Can Make Leaders Look less Effective", *Harvard Business Review*, September 2017.

298 Jim Collins, *Good to Great: Why some companies make the leap ... and others don't*, Random House, 2001.

299 Goffee and Jones, 2006.

300 Kegan, R., and Lahey, L. L., *Immunity to Change: How to Overcome it and Unlock the Potential in Yourself and Your Organization*, Harvard Business Press, 2009.

301 Gurdjian, P, Halbeisen, T, and Lane, K., "Why leadership development programs fail", *McKinsey Quarterly*, January 2014

302 Gentry, B., "Derailment: How Successful Leaders Avoid It", *ASTD Leadership Handbook*, 2010.

303 Kaiser, R. B., and Curphy, G., "Leadership Development: The Failure of an Industry and the Opportunity for Consulting Psychologists", *Consulting Psychology Journal: Practice and Research*, volume 65, 2013.

304 Weaver, P., and Mitchell, S., "Lessons for Leaders from the People Who Matter: How Employees Around the World View Their Leaders", *DDI International*, 2012.

305 Clayson, D. E., "Student Evaluations of Teaching: Are They Related to What Students Learn? A meta-Analysis and review of the Literature", *Journal of Marketing Education*, volume 31, 2009.

306 Tosi, H. L., et. al., "How Much Does Performance Matter? A Meta-Analysis of CEO Pay Studies", *Journal of Management*, volume 26, 2000.

307 Lowrey, A., "Even Among the Richest of the Rich, Fortunes Diverge", *New York Times*, February 11, 2014.

308 Cooper, M. J., Gulen, H., and Rau, P. R., "Performance for Pay? The Relationship Between CEO Incentive Compensation and Future Stock Price Performance", *Social Science Research Network*, November 2016.

Made in the USA
Lexington, KY
20 March 2018